Advance Praise for

A Boy's Passage

"Fathers everywhere should celebrate this significant book and what it will do for their families. The author has focused on a neglected area of fathering, highly significant in other cultures but sadly lacking in our own. I appreciate the tone of this book, which does not lay a guilt trip on fathers for what they have not done, but lovingly encourages them into some practical ways to have a life-changing time of bonding with their sons. I highly recommend this book to fathers around the world."

—V. Gilbert Beers, Ph.D.,
best-selling author of over one hundred books for children,
contributor to the *Life Application Bible* and the *TouchPoint Bible*

"With the manly sensitivity and spirituality that could only come from a father, Brian Molitor has given us a prescription that is both practical and needed. The seeds of a significant national movement are in this work."

—Jeff Wright, president of Urban Ministries

"Filled with uplifting personal experiences, *A Boy's Passage* expresses the responsibility we have as parents to prepare our sons to be men of God. Brian Molitor not only gives insight into the necessity of this transition celebration, but he also provides ideas on ways to prepare for such an event. A great tool for understanding our role in the spiritual development of our young men."

—Kathleen B. Jackson,
founder and publisher of *The Godly Business Woman Magazine*

"A wonderful, motivational book to help a dad understand his God-given role in shaping his son, this book is far more than simply an excellent read. What you have in your hand is a complete strategic business plan. The goal is to help you understand the mission, the objectives, and the step-by-step tactics to insure successful fatherhood. The dividend is a happy, fulfilled, and godly son. What could possibly be more valuable?"

—Robert Wolgemuth,
author of the notes in the best-selling *Devotional Bible for Dads*

"If every parent adopted the creative ideas contained in this book, we would not have the crisis in male leadership we have today. I found myself in tears as I read his account of the importance of giving every son a right of passage into adulthood. I realized the impact of my own lack of formal recognition of my entry into adulthood. Who knows what a difference a book like this could have made."

—Os Hillman, president of Marketplace Leaders,
author of *TGIF: Today God Is First*

"To say *A Boy's Passage* is absolutely captivating and inspiring is an understatement. Molitor's concept could truly make a difference for an untold number of lives."

—Tina Coonce, cofounder of TCT Television Network

A Boy's Passage

A BOY'S PASSAGE

Celebrating Your Son's Journey *to* Maturity

BRIAN D. MOLITOR

SHAW

WATERBROOK
PRESS

A Boy's Passage
A SHAW BOOK
PUBLISHED BY WATERBROOK PRESS
2375 Telstar Drive, Suite 160
Colorado Springs, Colorado 80920
A division of Random House, Inc.

All Scripture quotations, unless otherwise indicated, are taken from the *Holy Bible, New International Version®*. NIV®. Copyright © 1973, 1978, 1984 by International Bible Society. Used by permission of Zondervan Publishing House. All rights reserved. Scripture quotations marked (NKJV) are taken from the *New King James Version*. Copyright © 1982 by Thomas Nelson, Inc. Used by permission. All rights reserved. Scripture quotations marked (KJV) are taken from the *King James Version*.

Details in some anecdotes and stories have been changed to protect the identities of the persons involved.

ISBN 0-87788-112-X

SHAW BOOKS and its circle of books logo are registered trademarks of WaterBrook Press, a division of Random House, Inc.

Library of Congress Cataloging-in-Publication Data
Molitor, Brian D., 1952–
   A boy's passage : celebrating your son's journey to maturity / Brian D. Molitor.— 1st ed.
   p. c.m.
   ISBN 0-87788-112-X (pbk.)
   1. Teenage boys—Religious life. 2. Initiation rites—Religious aspects—Christianity.
3. Maturation (Psychology)—Religious aspects—Christianity. I. Title: Celebrating your son's journey to mature manhood. II. Title.

BV4541.3 .M64 2001
248.8'32—dc21   00-050326

Printed in the United States of America
2001—First Edition

10 9 8 7 6 5 4 3 2 1

To my grandfather,
Henry Albert Molitor

⟨⟩

This book is dedicated to the greatest man I have ever known, my grandfather.

Grandpa, you always had time to teach the important things in life. At your side, I learned how to catch a fish, how to hunt, and how to build the most marvelous creations out of wood.

The hours we spent together in northern Michigan are etched deeply in my mind. I still marvel at how you always knew just where to go to find a bluegill, bass, partridge, or white-tailed deer.

You took time with your grandchildren and made each one feel as if they were the only kid in the world. When I made mistakes, you helped me fix them. You never yelled; instead, you just had me try again. It was so clear that you lived for your children and grandchildren, not for yourself.

The scars on your body told of your sacrifice for your country in "the war to end all wars." Other people sometimes stared, but to me you were the most handsome man on earth. I took note that, despite your pain, you never complained and you never gave up.

Grandpa, when your time on earth was through and God took you home, my heart shattered into a million pieces. It took years for that same God to put the pieces back together.

I'm glad he did. I still miss you more than you could ever know.

I have a family of my own now. I sure wish you could have gotten to know them.

My wife, Kathleen, is the best thing that ever happened to me this side of heaven. She sticks with me through all of life's ups and downs. She's beautiful, both outside and inside.

I've got some children, too. Christopher is my oldest. He's a son other dads dream of. He is strong, smart, and good-looking. Best of all, he loves God with all his heart.

My next son, Steven, is a man after your own heart. Grandpa, he can make anything, fix anything, and work better than most men I know. His sense of humor keeps our family from taking life too seriously. I wouldn't trade him for anyone. God has a big plan for Steven.

Next comes Jenifer. God must have known that we couldn't handle three boys in a row. She is the most precious child you could ever imagine. She is tall and lovely. Her heart is so tender toward her mom and dad. Jeni is love personified and ministers to me with her smile.

My youngest son is Daniel Elijah. Grandpa, he is made just like you. He is strong and gentle at the same time. He is still young enough to want to just sit on my lap and talk. When we talk, I teach him about important things. Like how to catch a fish and how to hunt. And how to build things out of wood. At times, I tell him about his great-grandpa Henry and what it is like to become a man.

Thanks, Grandpa, for allowing God to use you in such a powerful way in my life.

Contents

A Word to Women

I need to share my heart with you about this book. I wrote it primarily to light a fire under the men of our nations. Men have so often left important matters—spirituality, child rearing, and mentoring our sons and daughters—for someone else to handle. The problem is that no one else can pick up our God-given responsibilities. As a result, you have suffered, our children have suffered, and while we may try to hide it, we men have suffered. That is about to change. As he said in the book of Malachi, God is turning the hearts of the fathers to their children and the hearts of the children to their fathers.

I ask you to read this book prayerfully and carefully. It holds keys as to why the men in your life act the way they do. It holds keys to your son's future as a mature man. It is a book about how we can help our sons, grandsons, and neighbors' sons grow up to accept their God-given callings as men.

So as you read, please don't feel slighted or undervalued. You are not. I simply wrote what was needed to awaken us all to our need to refocus attention on our precious young men. There is no message here, hidden or overt, that boys are better, more special, or more highly valued than girls in any way. Believe me, if my daughter, Jenifer, had been born first, this book would be titled *A Girl's Passage.*

Please join me in praying that men get the message that we must do more than just bring our sons into this world. We must also launch them into their manhood and walk with them every step of the way.

PREFACE

Our world today is filled with many crises. Wars, crime, moral decay, poverty, political scandal, drug abuse, and divorce are just a few of the seemingly insurmountable problems that steal our innocence and haunt our lives.

Many fight this trend toward societal disaster by whatever means they can. Every counselor, pastor, priest, politician, and parent that has ever taken a stand for righteousness helps hold the line of decency. Yet an honest review of the facts shows that while our society may win an occasional skirmish and even a battle or two, we are still losing the war.

Most people involved in this fight recognize that to reverse this negative trend we must address our problems' causes *before* they explode into crises. Failure to do so condemns us to years of just trying to suppress symptoms. Violence, rage, abuse, hopelessness, and breakdown of relationships are clearly seen in action, yet the root cause of these outward manifestations of human pain lies hidden deep within the soul.

My quest for answers to society's recurring problems began in earnest when my first son, Christopher, was born. As he grew, and his brothers and sister followed, my wife Kathleen and I wanted to empower them with hope, faith, and integrity; we wanted them to approach life by design and not by default. To do so, we recognized that we needed to strengthen them from the inside out.

Kathy and I acknowledged that the foundational answer to society's plight is first found in a personal relationship with God and in living according to the guiding principles found in the Bible. However, we also realized that entering into a relationship with God was just the first step of a fulfilled life. After that, a person's heart, character, and view of the world must continue to be formed or, better yet, transformed. Sadly, in our society today much of this work is being done after the fact. Rather than investing a dozen or so years preparing, mentoring, and encouraging our young people, we spend lifetimes trying to bring restoration, reconciliation, and healing to broken adults.

As my wife and I wrestled with these issues, we came to one simple conclusion: To reverse our society's downward spiral and to become victorious with the next generation, we had to impart a sure sense of identity in our children when they were still young. Kathy and I had particular interest in reaching young *men* as we saw Christopher approach adolescence and manhood.

It became clear that the heart of a man must receive instruction, love, and mentoring at the proper time if we are to turn the tide of crises in our world. These are the same men who will start wars or stop them, commit crimes or solve them, build families or destroy them. We must not allow one more child to drift into an uncertain future questioning his manhood. The stakes are too high, the potential losses too great.

I wrote this book to help us understand our sacred duty of raising our children to love God, their neighbors, and themselves so that our families and our nations may be healed. While the primary thrust of this book deals with young people, it also provides strategies for healing older men who lacked support in their early years. It will give you a strategy for doing your part and an assurance that others will do theirs.

God bless you, strengthen you, and encourage you as, together, we begin to reclaim what we never should have lost in the first place—the hearts of our children.

ACKNOWLEDGMENTS

There are many people I want to thank for their support, encouragement, contributions, wise counsel, and prayers.

Thanks to my wife Kathleen and our children, Christopher, Steven, Jenifer, and Daniel. Your love, support, and patience bring out the very best in me. You have captured my heart and taught me the meaning of home.

A special thanks to both sets of grandparents in our family: Bob and Jinny Molitor, and Jim and Betty Hayes. God used your love and guidance to bless our marriage and the next generation that bears your likeness. Now that we are parents, Kathy and I finally understand the sacrifice you made for your children. You have our gratitude, love, and devotion forever.

Deep appreciation to my favorite basketball coach, Roger Little, for his words of encouragement at just the right time. Many years ago God used you to help equip me for my life's work. Coach, I never quit, just like you told me.

Thanks to our team here at Molitor International's Power of Agreement Network that has been so supportive during this project. At the top of the list are John and Ann Bennett, Dick Eagan, Joel Freeman, Karen Spickerman, Jan Clarkson, Harry Marcus, Ric Suitor, Ron Ferguson, Ray Charles, and Linda Neuman. Thanks to Ric Olson and Trevor Knoeson, my partners in IBICC. You have all enriched my life and held up my arms more than you know.

I am most grateful for the many old and new friends that caught the vision of this book. They include Bradley Stuart, Dale Neill, Bill Watkins, Ron Ives, John Trent, and Joan Guest. I am also thankful for the people at WaterBrook that worked so hard to bring this project to completion. Don Pape, Elisa Fryling, and the rest of the crew have been great!

I want to say a special thanks to James Glenn, a precious friend that truly sticks closer than a brother. James, God sent us halfway around the world together more than once, and each time it was a grand adventure. Isn't it just like God to take a black man from the streets of Detroit and a white man from the woods of northern Michigan and make us an inseparable team? James, thank you for standing with me through all of the spiritual battles that have come. At times your buddy was wounded, tired, and about to give up when you came along, broke through the enemy's ranks, and pulled me out. Thanks, brother.

Thanks to all the men that attended the celebrations for my sons. Your zeal and commitment to the next generation of young men lit a fire within me that God turned into this book.

CHAPTER 1

PORTRAITS OF PASSAGE

The birth of a child. Few moments in life hold as much wonder, excitement, and promise. Months of anticipation and anxiety are quickly eclipsed as the baby miraculously appears. The new daughter or son fills a home with marvelous warmth.

From that moment on, life is never the same for any member of the family. By perfect design, the child looks to his mother and father to provide everything he needs to survive and grow during the early years. But that soon changes.

Days rush by and turn into years. Your boy's once tiny frame fills with muscle, and his mind fills with dreams. His bicycle trips around the block transcend into business trips around the world. All too soon, the baby has grown and begins to leave his own mark on history.

Throughout the process, parents do their level best to equip their son with all he needs to succeed. Nutrition, education, transportation, lectures, and love—all have been liberally supplied. Surely this is sufficient for him to prosper.

Or is it?

If these basics are all a boy needs to succeed, then why are so many males in our society today struggling with finding purpose, identity, and manhood itself? Why are so many men, young and old, depressed or anxious about life? Why are there so many horror stories involving crime, teen sex, drug and alcohol abuse, gangs, murder, and suicide?

Modern "experts" have studied these questions for years but offer no lasting answers. Our young men's lives continue to disintegrate at an alarming rate. Since the tide has not turned, we must be missing something. What is it? Do our sons need more government programs, more money, better schools, stricter punishment, enhanced youth ministries, or in-depth counseling sessions? Perhaps.

However, we can find help by looking to other societies, past and present, to discover a powerful secret of individual and national success. This secret is revealed as we study cultures that have long helped their sons' transitions into mature manhood by design rather than by default. Let's begin our cultural journey by visiting a tribe of eastern Africa…

THE MAASI: WALKING TOWARD DESTINY

Young Sidimo huddled against the cold night air. The small fire warmed his skin and brought comfort to his soul. His body was tired, but his mind raced with thoughts of what dawn would bring. Tomorrow was his special day. Tomorrow he would follow the path his father and other fathers of the Maasi tribe had walked for countless generations. Tomorrow, in the presence of the elders, Sidimo would become a man.

Thunder rolled far in the distance and lightning crashed around the sacred mountain, *Oldoinyo le Engai,* the Mountain of God. Young Sidimo strained his eyes to catch a glimpse of the majestic peaks that rose high into the ebony sky. Deep in his soul, he prayed that *Engai*—the God of his people—would be pleased with him.

The East African veldt was suddenly alive with the sounds and smells he'd known from early childhood. Powerful emotions surged through Sidimo as he heard the roar of a mighty lion not far away. A strange mixture of fear and exhilaration flooded his mind as he remembered the first time he heard that terrible sound. As a child, he'd been sleeping in his family's hut when a great lion leaped over the thorn fence to grab one of his family's prized calves. His father had fearlessly grabbed a spear and rushed outside to challenge the beast. At the sight of his father, the lion dropped the calf and retreated into the night.

Go ahead and roar, Simba, thought Sidimo. *One day I will meet you with a spear of my own, and you will flee. For when I pass the test tomorrow, I will become a man like my father!*

Sleep eluded Sidimo as his thoughts leapt about like nervous gazelles. This night was just as his father had told him it would be. Mysterious. Adventurous. Sobering. More exciting than any other night in his young life. This was the time when his past, present, and future all came together.

Sidimo thought of the items he'd left behind when he entered the jungle to begin his rite of passage. He remembered how his father had instructed him to discard all the possessions associated with his childhood. He must not retain the ornaments and trappings of a boy if he truly wanted to become a man. His father was so wise. Sidimo remembered the many hours he sat with him and the other elders to learn the ways of a man. For many generations, the elders of the tribe had taught the younger members that honesty, courage, loyalty, and personal responsibility were virtues associated with true men. Some of the elders' teachings were deeply spiritual and others dealt with the issues of sexuality, marriage, and even how to survive in the sometimes harsh environment of eastern Africa.

Sidimo stirred the fire and reflected on the many preparations of the past two months. Last week he had successfully raided a beehive and filled his cowhide container to the top with precious honey. With it his mother had made the traditional honey beer the elders would drink after the ceremony to honor Sidimo's bravery. Even now the liquid was chilling in a calabash gourd inside his mother's hut. The flowing ostrich plumes that would soon adorn his headdress were safely stored there as well.

His mental inventory completed, Sidimo took momentary solace in the fact that all was finally ready for his transition into manhood. With great joy he visualized the new hut that had been constructed for his triumphant return from his circumcision ceremony. Sidimo was more than willing to endure a few moments of pain for a lifetime of honor.

In the next instant his thoughts raced forward, anticipating what would happen when dawn broke over the low hill in the east. *I will walk to the center of the village where the elders will be waiting. I will then take my seat and sit straight as a spear,* thought Sidimo. *All of the other men of my village will surround me. My favorite uncle will take his position behind me to give me strength as the sharp blade cuts into my flesh. I will not cry out—I will not even blink at the sight of my blood as it spills on the ground. For if I were to "kick the knife" and show cowardice, my family would be disgraced. We would be spat upon and no one would eat the food prepared for the celebration!*

"No!" Sidimo shouted. He was startled by the sound of his voice as it shattered the stillness of the African night. A smile then grew from the grimace on his young face, and peace returned to his mind.

My name means, "He is able." No, I will not cry out, and soon the pain will be over, and my family will cheer. Only then will my mother be allowed to bring the milk she has collected so that both the knife and I may be cleansed. Then my relatives will say to me, "Get up, Sidimo! Get up! You are now a man!" But I will not move until they assemble to present many cattle to me so that I can begin my own herd.

Afterward, my uncle will lead me to the safety of my mother's hut. There I will stay until I am healed. When I have regained my strength, I will proudly walk through the village to my new hut where I will start a family of my own. It is there that someday I will share the ways of the Maasi with my own children. I will tell my sons of this night and of how their father became a man.

For the next few hours, Sidimo sat very still and gazed into the fire until all that remained were a few scattered embers. He noted that the fire seemed unwilling to relinquish its last moments but finally surrendered to the inevitable. Sidimo felt no sense of loss at the passing of the small fire. Soon the huge crimson sun rising over the low hills in the east replaced the fire's gentle glow. As the warmth of the new day touched Sidimo's face, he rose and walked toward his destiny.

THE LAKOTA: VISION QUESTING FOR MANHOOD

Worlds away and decades before, another boy, White Fox, had sat alone in the darkness. He kept a silent and lonely vigil atop a mountain in the territory that is now called South Dakota. Chilling winds blew raven-colored hair across his weathered face. Clad only in a buckskin loincloth, this young member of the Lakota tribe sat in the stillness and waited. His thin frame was weakened from the hours he'd spent purifying his body in the sweat lodge and from his days of fasting before he ascended the mountain. Normally, hunger pains would have sent White Fox on a quest for food. However, the ache in his belly served to remind him of how important tonight was. He knew that what happened this night would set the course for the rest of his life. This was the night of his vision quest. For generations the young men of his tribe had come to this place to earnestly seek the will of the Great Spirit for their lives.

White Fox could feel the strength of those who had come here before him as he called out to his creator. *Oh, Great Spirit,* prayed White Fox as a wolf's eerie howl pierced the night. *Come and show me the vision for my life. Why have you given me breath? What is my purpose for being?* For now, he heard no answers, only the sounds of the night.

The young man's heartfelt questions soon gave way to quiet reflections on his childhood. He vainly searched his memory for an image of his father, but none came to his mind. White Fox could only recall the story of when he was scarcely two seasons old, a band of renegades had raided his village. All of the braves fought valiantly against the invaders, but several were mortally wounded. While his father was defending his family, a lance pierced his side and he died. He had willingly died so that others could live. When White Fox was older, he learned that every member of his tribe had mourned the loss of his father, a man regarded as a great chief who sacrificed his life for others.

The boy's heart ached for the strong touch of his father's hand upon his shoulder. His brown eyes turned toward the heavens, and he spoke again. This time, there was no shout, only a quiet, pleading whisper. *Great Spirit, why was he taken away? Who will fill this canyon that I feel deep in my heart?*

Soon his swirling thoughts found refuge in a pleasant place. Bittersweet tears welled up in his eyes as he thought of his mother's love for him. She had been the one to watch over him for more than a decade. Despite the hardships of fending for her family, she had made sure that White Fox learned how to become respected among the tribe.

Others had rallied around him as well. Throughout the years, his father's friends had treated him as their own son. Early on, they had shown White Fox how to ride the painted ponies that seemed to fly across the grasslands. He remembered the time that one of the elders had presented him with his first bow and a quiver of arrows. Fondly he recalled the many evenings he would go with the elders to hunt for deer near the watering holes on the plains. As they walked together, these elders taught him about the ways of a warrior. They would sit with him for hours and speak of the changes that he would experience on his journey to manhood. From these times he learned about the importance of a man's honor and the responsibilities of community leadership.

Suddenly, the vision he had been seeking exploded before him. A smile broke across his broad face. His vision came riding upon the words his mother had spoken to him many years ago. They flashed across his mind like lightning. "Someday," she had said, "you will take your father's place and lead others in our tribe."

"Great Spirit!" White Fox shouted. "I now understand why you have given me breath. I am to walk in the ways of my father and the teachings of my mother. Now that he is gone, I am to take my father's place! At first light, I will return to my lodge and tell my family of my vision. Tomorrow will be a most special day for me! Yes, tomorrow will be most special."

The Ancient Romans: Honoring a New Citizen

Centuries earlier another boy waited impatiently for the ceremony that would catapult him into manhood. Young Marcus stood on the balcony of his family's villa that overlooked the Seven Hills of Rome. A warm breeze carried the faint scent of the sea into his nostrils and reminded him of times of play on the sandy Italian shores. Carefully cultivated fields flanked red-brick roads that snaked through the countryside. For years Marcus had watched these fields change with the seasons. Men who understood such things kept a continuous vigil over those fertile lands. They meticulously planted seed in spring, then carefully weeded and pruned and watered during the summer. Finally, in the fall, the precious crops were harvested and transformed into the life-giving bread that sustained the Roman people. From his vantage point, Marcus could see the city in all its splendor.

The boy's eyes soon locked upon the soldiers of the Praetorian Guard as they paraded through the narrow streets. These were special men of the emperor's garrison who had proven themselves worthy to guard the very heart of the empire, Rome itself.

To the north Marcus saw groups of politicians filing into the great forum for another round of heated debates about matters of state. Marcus was proud to know that his father was among them.

He continued to scan the vast city and marvel at what men had been able to build. He identified the extensive aqueducts that brought water to Rome's many public baths. In the marketplace, he saw hundreds of street vendors noisily trying to entice citizens and slaves alike to buy their wares. Fish from the sea, cattle from the fields, and household goods made of bronze, wood, and clay were sold throughout the day. The air was filled with the sounds and colors and dust of the many visitors who came from the four corners of the earth just to experience this great city.

Marcus never seemed to tire of watching the ways of his city. It was always so alive. However, today was different; he didn't linger long at the balcony. Instead, he withdrew to the quiet of his room and pondered what the next twenty-four hours would bring.

He knew that this was the month of March, and tomorrow the festival of Bacchus would begin. This meant that the special coming-of-age ceremonies would be held for every citizen's son who had reached his fourteenth birthday during the previous year. Tomorrow Marcus would go with his family to the great Forum and assemble with countless other families who knew the value of this rite of passage.

As part of the ceremony, Marcus would discard his boyish neck charms and the clothing of a child. He would also go with his father to the barber and be shaved for the first time. Following that, he would be registered as a citizen of Rome. As a citizen, Marcus would enjoy all the privileges and responsibilities that accompanied such an honor. At the end of the public ceremony, Marcus and his peers would offer sacred honey cakes on the altar of Bacchus.

Later in the day, many people would gather in his father's home for more celebration—celebration to commemorate his entry into manhood. There would be much eating and drinking, as the grand occasion would last for nearly a week. During that time, his father's friends would come and bring him some wonderful gifts.

Marcus marveled that such an occasion would be held in his honor. But even more wonderful than the party or the many gifts was the realization that, from that day forward, everyone would treat him differently. They would no longer see him as a child but rather as a man.

Tomorrow I will become a man, Marcus said to himself as his mind's eye flooded with pictures of the soon-coming event. *Then I will accompany my father when he goes into the city. I will walk beside him and even hear his speeches at the great assembly.*

Marcus knew that his father, a senator, was to address the assembly that day about the growing problems facing their nation. More than once, his father's calm demeanor and sage advice had been instrumental in forming a consensus among the politicians gathered at the forum. Even the great Emperor Augustus took note of what his father had to say.

Marcus's thoughts were interrupted by the quiet voice of Demetrius, his father's most trusted servant. "Marcus, it's time for your lessons."

Marcus tried to calculate how many times he'd heard those words over the past fourteen years. Most mornings since he was very young, he had met with Demetrius to learn about history, geometry, geography, astronomy, boxing, wrestling, music, and philosophy. Recently he had begun to study public speaking in preparation for his future. He wanted to become a senator, just like his father.

Demetrius taught Marcus about spiritual things as well. The boy recalled the hushed tones his mentor had used to describe the many gods that ruled over the nation, telling him how a man's conduct was under constant celestial scrutiny. Demetrius had also taken special care to explain the intricacies of citizenship and loyalty to one's country. Manliness, hygiene, the marriage vows, and even the mysteries of the marriage bed were all subjects of the young man's education.

Such waves of memories washed gently upon Marcus's mind and then slowly receded. For a brief moment, a touch of sadness invaded the boy's room. This was the last day of his childhood. *No longer will I wear the necklace of a boy,* thought Marcus. *No longer will I dress in the garments of my childhood. From now on, I will wear the clothing of a man. My whole life is about to change.* At tomorrow's ceremony, when his father would place a special toga over Marcus's shoulders and slip a ring on Marcus's finger, everything would change. Marcus was amazed that in less than twenty–four hours, his words would be measured by the same standard as his father's words.

Without warning, the touch of sadness in his soul grew into a whirlwind of self-doubt. "What if I fail?" Marcus blurted out. "What if I cannot remember all that I am to do as a man? What if…?"

"Marcus," called the soothing voice of Demetrius. "It is time."

Those three words were enough to reduce the storm in Marcus's mind to a mere breeze. He realized he would not have to make the journey through manhood alone. After all, the gods watched over the conduct of men, and he had learned his lessons well. Marcus would do his best, and that would be enough. "Yes," said Marcus quietly, as he donned the clothing of a boy for the last time. "It is time."

THE JEWS: OBSERVING A SACRED TRADITION

Traditions, pondered David, a young Jewish boy of Europe in the late 1920s. *I feel sorry for people who have no traditions. They make life worth living. My father says they are like mile markers on our passage through time. Yes, traditions are very good things.*

This young man had learned the lesson well, despite the many distractions of living in Eastern Europe after the big war. Life for all people was still very unsettled. There were homes to be rebuilt, businesses to reopen, and the dead to be mourned. Through it all, David's family had held closely to each other, to their God, and to their traditions.

Tomorrow I will celebrate becoming a man, thought David with a smile. *Tomorrow I will become a bar mitzvah—a son of the commandment. But I have no time to think about it now, for I must go and help my father at his shop.*

Young David left the small house he shared with his father, mother, two sisters, and the three cousins who had been orphaned by the war. His feet flew down the street, and he soon found himself at the door of his father's shop.

While still standing outside, David recalled happy days spent at the shop watching his father work. Often the two of them did not speak but just enjoyed the closeness of their fellowship. Sometimes they would joke with each other. David remembered that often his father would tell him a funny story. His father also told him that God trusted all watchmakers, because the Almighty allowed them to "hold time in their hands." David and his father would both laugh, even though they had shared the same story many times. They just loved being together. At other times, his father would teach David about his business and the value of work itself. He often said that a man must learn to work and work to learn—in equal portions. This way a man is ready for whatever God brings him to do in this life.

As David turned the front door's ornate handle, he was pleased to think that his father's door was always open to him. With a twist of his wrist, he entered his father's world of clocks, watches, and wonder. The tiny bell above the shop door announced his arrival as he walked inside. David was proud that his father was a watchmaker. His mother often boasted that her husband was the finest watchmaker in all Europe.

Once inside, David greeted his father and announced that he had finished his studies for the day. Then he sat up on the tall stool next to his father's workbench and began to disassemble a broken watch. His fingers weren't as skilled as his father's, but he was learning with each new day.

As he worked, his thoughts drifted back to one of his earliest memories of his father. It was David's first day of school, and his father had wrapped him in a traditional prayer shawl and carried him to his classroom. *I was so proud that my father carried me in,* thought David. *He is not a big man, but his arms and hands are so strong. I knew he would never drop me.*

David chuckled to himself as he recalled how his teacher would write on the blackboard with honey instead of chalk. *When I would say a letter, my teacher took my finger and traced it. Then I got to lick the honey. It made me want to learn all the more. I liked that tradition!*

With all of the clocks and watches marking time around him, it was difficult for David not to think about tomorrow. He felt a mixture of excitement and anxiety at the thought of his special day, his day of bar mitzvah. He put down his tools without realizing it.

His father's voice invaded the stillness of his thoughts. "David, that watch won't be fixed by itself. Are you thinking about tomorrow or just daydreaming?"

"Tomorrow, father. I was thinking about tomorrow," acknowledged David.

"Don't worry, my son. During this past year, you have studied hard to prepare for your ceremony, and you will do fine. Think of the many times we have gone to the synagogue together. You have learned the service and understand how to read our Hebrew language. Remember, David, you will repair more than watches during your lifetime. This whole world is in great need of repair, and God has much for you to do. He will be with you."

His father's warm smile gave David some temporary relief from the nagging thoughts in his mind. David knew that tomorrow he would become an adult and would be responsible for his own conduct. *As an adult, I must become a* mensch—*a generous, honorable, and compassionate person,* he said to himself. This was a big task, but he knew that the sacred writings of the Talmud promised that a bar mitzvah receives an extra soul as he becomes more closely connected with God. David was cautiously confident that this spiritual connection would help him overcome the habits of boyhood.

In his mind, David considered what he had to perform tomorrow. *First, in the morning, I will dress in my new suit and eat a light breakfast with my family. Then, according to tradition, I and my family will walk together to the synagogue where we will be seated in the front row of chairs. At that point, I will put on my* tallit, *my prayer shawl, and try to relax.*

Suddenly, it's as if David is actually there. He raises his eyes to the platform and sees the rabbi looking directly at him. The rabbi's friendly nod helps calm David's stomach.

The young man then glances to his right and sees his father sitting proud and straight. The look in his eyes suggests that he is reflecting on his own special day, which occurred over thirty years ago.

David's mother gently whispers to him, "My son, you are well prepared. You cannot fail! Go and do your best." Her hand brushes his cheek, and the look on her face speaks of countless days and nights when she proudly held him in her arms. Without a further word, her smile communicates to David that over the past thirteen years any sacrifice she made for him was well worth it. No, she would not trade her young *son of the commandment* for anything in the world.

Soon the ceremony begins. It is filled with rich sounds and traditions. A cantor opens the main part of the service with a melodious prayer called the *Borchu*. Then the ark is opened and the precious Torah—the Word of God—is brought forth. Next, his father and some men who are close to his family take turns speaking forth blessings and reading from the Torah.

Now it is time for David to ascend the platform. As his trembling hands grasp the scroll that he will read from, his eyes scan the crowd assembled in the synagogue. They have come to celebrate with him. It is tradition. A good tradition.

David pronounces the blessing and then reads from the ancient documents. His voice is strong and his hands have become steadier. When he has completed his reading, he gives the *Dvar Torah*—his very first sermon based on the Torah reading. His words are a mix of boyish innocence and manly conviction. When he is finished, he descends the platform and rejoins his family.

A single stately tear winds its way down his father's cheek and disappears into the thick black beard. His mother casts a glance that says "I knew he could do it" at relatives and friends in the rows behind her. Then…

"David?" his father's call startles him back into the present. "My son, that watch is just as broken as it was ten minutes ago." Tapping his temple with his index finger, his father asks, "Have you returned to the synagogue?"

"Yes, father," David answers. This time he was a bit embarrassed to admit that he was captured with the thoughts of tomorrow.

His father laughed that special laugh—the one that came from deep in his belly. "Come then, David. The sun is about to go down on today and we must close up the shop. Here at work, we will have many days like today, but there will only be one special day for you like tomorrow. And there is much to be done to prepare. Even now, your mother is cooking for your party that will follow the ceremony. Everyone will be there. You will receive many presents, and we will eat and we will sing and we will dance. My son, it will be a day you will never forget!"

As they stepped outside the shop, David stood beside his father and waited for him to lock the door as he had so many times before. However, today his father did something different. He reached for his son's hand and dropped something into his palm. David was surprised to see that his father had given him a new key on a silver chain.

"Today, David," his father said with a smile. "Today, *you* lock the door. After all, God willing, this will be your shop someday."

David gripped the key tightly, and with his father at his side, he locked the door. Then the two of them began the walk home together as they had done so many times before.

For them it was a tradition.

A good tradition.

The Modern Way: Stumbling Toward...*What?*

Sunday morning. Nine-thirty.

Jason sat on the corner of the bed and tried to shake the sleep from his head. He still felt somewhat strange waking up at his father's house, despite the fact that he'd spent nearly every other weekend there since the divorce. Outside, the cold north wind rattled Jason's window and reminded him that the seasons were changing again.

For an instant, Jason's thoughts flashed back to the Sunday mornings when his parents were still together. He remembered sneaking into their bedroom and crawling in to snuggle with them as they slept. Memories of the feelings, sounds, and even pleasant smells of his dad's aftershave lotion and his mom's perfume flooded his senses and gave birth to a small smile. For a fleeting moment he was once again warm and happy and secure. With his mom on one side and his dad on the other, he felt as if nothing could ever go wrong. Not even the dreadful monsters that sometimes lurked in the shadows of his room at night could invade that sanctuary.

Dad would play that game where he would snore so loud, and I would pinch his nose, recalled Jason. *Then Mom would tickle me until I begged her to stop...although I really hoped she wouldn't.*

The sound of a truck roaring past the house brought Jason back to the present. His smile disappeared, and he felt a little silly to have thought about things from so long ago. *What difference does it make anyway?* he rationalized. *Live for today, right? That's what Dad says.*

Rising from the bed, Jason quietly shuffled to the bathroom. Today, the fair-weather friend of a mirror was on Jason's side. It showed that the biceps he was working so hard to build were starting to bulge a bit. The shadow on his upper lip was beginning to darken, and, mercifully, the pimple on his chin had begun to retreat. It seemed as if he were making progress in his quest to grow up.

As he made his way downstairs, Jason walked past the door to his father's room. It was always shut. As Jason entered the family room, he smelled old smoke and saw the leftover party food still scattered about. *Oh yeah,* remembered Jason. *Dad's party.*

The house seemed strangely quiet after last night's wild get-together. Some of his dad's friends had come over to celebrate his new promotion. Although his father had politely asked Jason to "keep a low profile" during the party, Jason couldn't help but overhear the festivities. From his room, he had heard the men offer many toasts to his dad. Jason remembered that one man with a deep, raspy voice kept repeating, "You finally made it, man! You finally made it!"

Jason poured some juice and, as he glanced about the kitchen, saw the calendar on his dad's refrigerator door. Barely visible among the many notes about business meetings, appointments, and garbage pickup days were some smudged pencil marks about Jason's birthday tomorrow. Several years ago Jason would have felt some real excitement about that fact. Birthdays meant presents. Birthdays meant CDs, video games, and new clothes.

But for Jason, birthdays had also come to mean disappointment. After nearly a decade and a half of birthdays, he wouldn't allow himself to get his hopes too high about his "special day."

What a joke, he thought. He now knew the pattern all too well. For the past three years, at least one of his parents had had a schedule conflict with his birthday. They were always so busy with work, social events, and, lately, weekends away to "find themselves." Often they would reschedule his birthday celebration rather than reschedule their meetings. For a while, Jason hadn't really minded. It seemed that the more hectic the year became, the bigger the presents he received. In the past, it seemed like a fair trade-off. But today, deep inside, he realized things were changing.

Jason didn't care if he got any presents this year on his "special day." Plastic, denim, and microchips no longer satisfied him. He just wished that his family could eat and talk together—just be together. *What would really make tomorrow special is if Dad would just sit and talk with me without always looking at his watch. That would be worth a hundred presents. A thousand presents.*

He felt that familiar I-can't-deal-with-this ache rising in his chest, so he quickly slammed the door of his heart. *It's just a stupid birthday, anyway. So what if I'm going to be a teenager. What's the big deal? Besides, some of the older kids in the neighborhood said they would throw me a real party tomorrow night. Those guys sure act crazy sometimes...*

He got dressed and went back into the family room where his dad's party had ended just a few hours earlier. Jason thought about how strange it was to call this room a "family" room, since there was never any family there. Stepping over the trash, he considered cleaning it all up, but he was unsure where to begin. Instead, he retrieved the backpack containing his school books and seated himself at the kitchen table to work on an assignment due the next day. *Most of my teachers are great,* he decided. *They really care about us. But, man, some of them are hard to follow.*

He recalled how at times school had become so confusing. Some subjects were in conflict with others, or at least that's how it seemed. One instructor taught that mankind was bad and that we should reduce the human population to avoid the further polluting of "Mother Earth." She made a point of calling creationism an ancient fairy tale and said she wouldn't waste class time discussing it. According to her, God did not exist. Instead, life began billions of years ago when some molecules came together and formed living beings. Over time, these single-celled beings evolved into higher states of life. Man was now the highest form of animal and would continue to become bigger, better, and brighter. Yet Jason had seen enough television news reports to doubt the notion that human beings, on their own, were becoming better or brighter in any way. It was all sort of bewildering.

Jason then recalled that midway through the second semester, a special speaker was invited to talk to the students about self-esteem. Evidently, school officials were alarmed at the increase in student violence, teen pregnancy, and the fact that three kids had committed suicide that year. The speaker had spent two hours trying to convince the students that they were "special" and that they were all really going to be "somebody" someday.

Let's see, Jason puzzled. *My one teacher says mankind is bad and that we sprang up from some mud a few zillion years ago. But that other guy said I am special and someday I will be somebody. How does that fit together? And if God doesn't exist, why does my football coach pray before each game? Who's right and who's wrong?*

Frustrated, Jason struggled to reconcile the conflicting messages he'd received about other issues, such as abortion, sex, and growing up. None of it was making much sense.

Mercifully, Jason heard his father open his bedroom door and then shuffle out to meet him. Despite the gray streaks in his dad's hair and his expanding waistline, Jason still thought his father was a wonderful sight to behold. He sincerely treasured what little time they had together.

"Hi Dad!" Jason said with a smile. "Man, I'm sure glad you're finally up. I've been thinking a lot lately and wanted to run some things past—"

"You know, Son," his dad interrupted in his most upbeat voice. "I've got some serious shopping to do before tomorrow. My new promotion came with a bonus, and I want to buy you something you'll really like. So, how about it? What do you want?"

Jason's heart began to crumble. "Dad, I really like what you buy me. But what I really want is just to hang out together. I'm growing up—I mean, I think I am growing—and I…"

"Oh, is that it?" his dad said nervously. "I know what you mean about time with your dad. My dad worked all the time, but I got used to it. Hey, we just spent the weekend together, didn't we? As far as the manhood thing, don't worry about it. Just look at the size of you! Manhood just…just…you know, just happens by itself. My dad never made a big deal out of it, and look how I turned out. Why, when I was your age…"

Jason didn't hear the rest of his dad's story. Minutes later, he sat silently in the car, waiting to be driven back to his mother's house.

His dad soon appeared and slid into the driver's seat. Backing the car out of the driveway, his father proudly asked, "What do you think of my yard? Isn't it beautiful? Of course, it doesn't just happen by itself. Takes hours each week, but it's worth it. Hey, a man isn't much of a man if he doesn't keep his yard looking great. Do you know what I mean, Son?"

Jason nearly missed his dad's question. A tear had slipped past his defenses, and he quickly spun his face away from his father. Soon the car pulled up in front of his mother's house and came to a halt on top of the piles of leaves Jason had raked into the street. The young man composed himself, slowly got out of the car, and poked his head through the passenger-side window to say good-bye.

"Well, so long, Dad," he said quietly. "I *will* see you tomorrow, right?"

"You bet, Son. I wouldn't miss your special day for the world. We're going to have some food and then your presents. It will be great! I'll be here at six, and I can stay until at least eight-thirty. Remember, it's your special…" Glancing at his watch, his dad exclaimed, "Wow, look at the time! I really need to get going." With that, he pulled the car into the street and sped away.

Although his father wasn't aware of it, his departure created a powerful vacuum behind him. The leaves Jason had carefully raked into neat piles were soon scattered. With one foot on the curb, Jason watched his father get smaller and smaller until he could see him no longer. Then Jason went inside and locked the door.

CHAPTER 2

BOYS TO MEN

My heart aches for Jason and the millions like him who must try to find the door to manhood and then travel the pathway to maturity by themselves. Unlike Sidimo, White Fox, Marcus, and David, many boys in contemporary society are lost in the shuffle of everyday life. Not only are wonderful opportunities to shape their character and destiny missed during the most formative years of their young lives, but their transition away from boyhood practically goes unnoticed. Today's boys rarely, if ever, learn from the adults closest to them what it means to become a man—or learn when they have become one. Instead, they are left to search for answers in movies, song lyrics, the often ill-informed perspectives of their peers, and the mixed, even contradictory, messages coming from other "grownups" around them. As a consequence, we have too many "Jasons" limping through life. They are confused, hurting, and feeling terribly incomplete.

In other cultures and eras, the message and making of manhood are straightforward. Older men and women from one generation pour themselves into the boys of the following generation. They teach, mentor, counsel, correct, love, listen to, and, in short, nurture these boys to prepare them for the responsibilities of manhood. In return, the youth are expected to grow into increasing responsibility, accountability, and concern for others.

As the boys' maturity grows, the adults in their lives empower them with increased freedom to make choices for themselves and their future families. By parental and communal design, each young man is provided excellent opportunities to become a productive member of his family and society. Young males are taught that manhood is much more than having the physical ability to make children. It is having the maturity to love, lead, teach, and nurture children. Further, the younger learn from their elders that mature men do not dominate or harm their wives; rather, they learn to love, protect, and nurture them as well. In due time, the cycle repeats itself, and these now mature men help others follow in their footsteps, thus retaining and building on the foundations of their culture.

Pursuing a Healthy Cycle of Maturity

This ongoing, cyclical pattern for building successful families and societies was noted by secular anthropologist Margaret Mead more than thirty years ago. In her book, *Male and Female: A Study of the Sexes in a Changing World,* she wrote:

> The human family depends on social inventions that
> will make each generation of males want to nurture
> women and children. Moreover, every known human
> society rests firmly on the learned nurturing behavior of

men. In all societies each new generation of young males needs to learn appropriate nurturing behavior.[1]

This truth has been well understood by many cultures throughout history. In stark and troubling contrast, our society has lost sight of what it takes to prepare young people to enter into responsible adulthood. Our abandonment of this sacred, time-tested cycle of maturity has led to countless problems for our culture, our families, and individual teens such as Jason.

It seems adults have become too preoccupied with nonessentials to effectively mentor, teach, and empower our sons and daughters as they grow up. As long as our personal comfort zone isn't invaded by some major youth tragedy, we tend to ignore the real needs of the young people in our homes, communities, schools, and churches. In today's world, it's just too easy for us to rush ahead with life, impervious to the teenage time bombs that will someday explode across the headlines of our newspapers.

I confess that before 1997 I rarely thought about the state of our teenagers and the long-term implications of neglecting their transition into adulthood. A news report about a teen who had gone over the edge might capture my attention momentarily, but the affect it had on me wouldn't linger for long. I found the report's accompanying statistics cold and devoid of any real meaning for my own life. High rates of suicide, teen pregnancy, crime, runaways, school dropouts, and drug

---

1. Margaret Mead, *Male and Female: A Study of the Sexes in a Changing World* (New York: Morrow, 1949).

and alcohol abuse among our youth were points of brief concern, but hardly causes for serious reflection. To me, these accounts were merely pieces of information rather than testimonies of ruined lives and wasted potential.

On those rare occasions when I did consider the plight of our youth, my thoughts only generated questions without answers. I wondered why "good" kids threw away their precious lives doing such stupid things. Why would any young man want to join a gang and risk bodily harm, imprisonment, or death? Why would such bright children take drugs to numb their fertile minds? What was wrong with *them?*

Over time, the increasing, often tragic, signs of our troubled youth caused me to wonder whether the problem wasn't more with *us* rather than *them*. I also began to question why so many people—myself included—were too busy to deal with these issues. Were we like Jason's father, too preoccupied with our own lives to hear the questions our young people were asking? I eventually came to a painful and unavoidable conclusion: What was wrong with *them* was rooted in what was wrong with *us*.

From this new perspective, I could see that my wife, Kathleen, and I were missing some key ingredients in our children's development. I just wasn't sure what they were.

MAKING IT A PERSONAL QUEST

In early 1997 the need to discover how we could help our children transition into adulthood became my personal quest. I felt a true sense of urgency as our oldest son, Christopher, was going to turn thirteen later that year. Kathleen and I wanted to do something significant to help make his birthday a turning point in his life. By God's grace, the answer came as I was returning from a trip to Pretoria, South Africa.

My close friend and long-time business associate, James Glenn, and I had been invited to South Africa to participate in an international Christian business conference. James is also pastor of a church in Saginaw, Michigan, and I was thrilled to have his company on this trip. Upon our arrival, we discovered that a kaleidoscope of fascinating people from all over the world were in attendance. James and I met with the president of Benin, Africa, and we worked with him to develop a plan to improve the quality of life for the five and a half million citizens of his fine nation. On our final day in Africa, I was honored to have the opportunity to address the conference's general assembly.

Despite our full schedule, I was preoccupied with thoughts of Christopher's upcoming special day, which then was approximately three weeks away. When the conference ended, James and I said good-bye to that beautiful land, boarded a plane, and collapsed into our seats. Before long, my friend drifted into a peaceful sleep while I pondered the significance of our trip.

Africa's wonderful, wild blur of colors and sounds provide an absolute feast for the senses. The cycles of life are evident everywhere. Newborn nations, like newborn antelope, learn to survive swiftly or die untimely deaths. Change is continuous. Today's national hero is tomorrow's scapegoat. Men's legacies are established or destroyed by a risky decision, a bold action, or a few words spoken at exactly the right or wrong time.

My visit there provoked many new questions about my own life's purpose. Thoughts about my family, personal legacies, and my oldest son's special day swirled within me. Even a brief reflection about my own mortality crept into the mix. Christopher wasn't the only one in our family who would have a birthday at the end of the month. I would reach the ripe age of forty-five on July 29. That fact alone led me to ponder some deep things about the future.

As our giant plane soared higher into the clouds, I began considering the whole issue of a person's legacy. I truly wanted to leave things here on earth better than I had found them, but I was unsure about how to accomplish that task. After numerous mental side trips around the subject, my thinking returned to my children. I began to realize that each person's legacy or reputation is comprised of two elements. One is *what we do with our own lives* while here on earth. Such things as the nature of our character, our contributions to society, our vocation, and our acts of service to others comprise a large portion of our legacy. The second component of legacy is based on *what our children do and what they become* during their time here on earth.

This issue of legacy and its connection with our children really challenged me. Especially when I considered how many young people were in trouble these days. Why don't we parents do something more about it? If our love and concern for our children are not motivation enough, why don't we act to protect our own reputations or legacies, which are so tied to our children's actions?

I wondered if there were things we parents were failing to do—things that actually *caused* our young people to stumble. More positively, I wondered if there were some basic things we could do to help our young people have the best possible opportunities for success. I used every moment that remained of my thirty-hour trip to sort through these issues until I finally arrived at few solid conclusions:

Conclusion #1: My Priorities Have to Change

As a typical "grown-up" male, I spent more time on my vocation, personal achievements, recreation, and activities with nonfamily members than I needed to. I owned my own business, had achieved some degree of financial stability, and was a published writer. I was doing a fair job building the personal side of my legacy ledger. So far, so good. But I was saddened to realize that I was falling short in both the quantity and quality of time needed to mentor my children to adulthood. That needed to change.

Conclusion #2: My Children Need More than Just Time in Order to Mature

Although I was a good provider for my family and spent considerable time with my children, I'd never clearly identified what they needed in order to make the transition into productive adults. Unintentionally, I had placed a higher priority on giving them brand-name basketball shoes than on giving them foundations upon which to build their lives. I finally saw that my lack of attention to this could cause some real harm to them later in their lives. I also realized that other parents were likely following an all-too-similar pattern with their own children.

Conclusion #3: I Must Be Intentional and Organized in My Approach to Changing the Situation

I started by making lists and action plans. I made a list of issues that could help our young people make the transition into adulthood. As I wrote down some of the basics, such as education, spiritual training, and supportive relationships at home, I struggled with a sense that something was still missing. Could there be a significant event, or a memorable moment, that marked the transition? Instantly, one item on my list—the rite of passage—exploded in my thinking.

ACKNOWLEDGING THE MISSING INGREDIENT

The rite of passage—our modern society's elusive, missing ingredient. It was something I hadn't thought much about before, and yet it now seemed so profound. The more I pondered the importance of a rite of passage in a young man's development, the more convinced I became that this was a key, not only to Christopher's future, but also to the healthy maturing of the other children in our society. Here is why.

For the most part, adults are well aware of the many problems plaguing our young people. However, I believe we've misdiagnosed the root cause of their troubling behavior. One of the most prominent words used to describe the baby boomers and following generations is *selfish*. While this term aptly describes many behaviors and attitudes, it doesn't go deep enough. It fails to uncover the genesis of their, no *our*, predicament.

As a business consultant, I've learned that the way we define a problem determines how the problem will be solved. The more accurate the definition, the better the opportunity to find effective solutions. The selfish label is too vague and almost always too simplistic to account for our seemingly endless problems. These include divorce, child abuse and abandonment, something-for-nothing lawsuits, personal aimlessness, emotional distress, and general lack of peace running rampant in our contemporary culture. Self-centeredness may partially explain the increase in some of these problems, but it doesn't suffice as an all-embracing explanation. More importantly, it doesn't get at the root cause of these problems.

As I have listened to the accounts of so many troubled boomers, busters, and Xers, I've concluded that a more foundational description of their condition can be summed up in a different word: *childishness.* Too many people today have never transitioned from children into adults, and they don't understand what prevents them from doing so. It's well documented that many of our young people haven't had the benefit of supportive family relationships, mentoring, a code of conduct, and foundations for maturity. I have no doubt that this lack has caused much of the negative behavior in our teens and young adults today.

However, even in "good" homes where these components exist, children may still increase in age without experiencing a corresponding increase in maturity. While they may avoid some of life's most obvious pitfalls, they lack purpose and direction and a clear picture of their own identity. They often retain many childlike fears, attitudes, and patterns of behavior well into adulthood. Many are haunted by a sense that *something* is still missing in their lives. That something is a rite of passage from childhood into adulthood. I need to underscore this point. The foundational reason childishness persists well into adulthood is because we do not create and implement transitional rites of passage for our youth.

As I looked deeper into this issue, I made a list of negative childish actions. Selfishness was definitely high on the list, followed by complaining, quitting when faced with a difficult situation, throwing temper tantrums, spewing threats of self-destruction, struggling with short attention spans, and demanding one's own way without regard for the needs of others. Sadly, while these actions are often seen in young children, the list also describes far too many "grown" men in our culture. For example, in a previous book I tell the story of a fifty-year-old production manager named Joe who fits the description of an angry child to a T. During his twenty-year reign of terror in the workplace, Joe continually bullied, belittled, and intimidated everyone under his supervision. Like children cornered in a school hallway, his employees cowered when Joe approached them. The reason? He would shout at, curse, and even threaten to physically harm any subordinate who dared challenge his authority. Joe's childish behavior continued until someone with greater power came along and stopped him. After patiently attempting to change Joe's behavior, Joe's boss fired him. You see, Joe was a child in a man's body.

We also see this childish pattern played out in even more destructive scenarios. Too many recent headlines have told the story of men who became frustrated with some aspect of their lives, so they lashed out in uncontrolled violence. Unable to deal with life's inevitable disappointments in a mature manner, some disgruntled men have stormed into the offices of their supervisors, attorneys, or stockbrokers and begun shooting everyone in sight. Like little boys who hit their playmates when they don't get their way, these men—adult in body but still children in so many other ways—use deadly force to impose their wills on the uncooperative.

Yet another manifestation of this childish mind-set exhibits itself when adult men abandon their commitments, especially in the family arena. When we were children, we always wanted new things. Toys, sports gear, even cars were all "better" if they were new. We not only enjoyed them but also wanted to show them off to our friends. When they lost their luster, broke, or became a bit outdated, we whined. We were unsatisfied with what had previously brought us so much pride and happiness. We then wanted to throw our "old" toys away and get new ones, believing that would make us happy—which, of course, the new toys did, but just for a little while. Then the cycle of dissatisfaction and the search for a new replacement would begin again, and always with the same temporary result.

Compare this childish practice with the modern-day approach to marriage. When a spouse gains a few pounds, doesn't agree with our opinions as readily as before, or begins to wane in outward beauty, many of us manifest the same type of childish behavior we did years ago. We lose interest and start desiring a "newer" model. Sadly, such men have never grown up. Unlike Sidimo or Marcus, no one ever lovingly challenged them to put down their childish things and pick up the mantle of manhood.

DEVELOPING A NEW MIND-SET

It's clear that the lack of an intentional transition into adulthood creates a variety of problems for men of all ages. In an attempt to compensate for the lack of a transitional event, some teens unknowingly create their own rites of passage by resorting to violence, drugs, alcohol, and sexual conquest to try to make their transition to adulthood. In the corporate world, some men in leadership positions use the authority of their job titles to threaten others into submission. Like bullies that stalk junior high schoolyards, these "grown" men live to verbally wrestle and pin their weaker opponents during staff meetings.

Often, men in their late thirties and forties stumble into what is commonly called a midlife crisis. During this time, men are consumed with a desire to search for meaning and identity in their lives. This sounds strangely familiar to the vision quest that White Fox undertook at age fourteen.

In today's society, men seem to have a difficult time settling in to life. Many struggle with a Peter Pan syndrome. They don't want to grow up, and yet they realize they were created for a higher purpose than endless play in never-never land. How sad to see men at the end of their lives, estranged from their families, still unsure about spiritual realities, still questioning the reason for their own existence, still wondering if they have succeeded in growing into manhood. Just as sad are the countless families whose teens fall into the predictable traps along the road of life because they don't know what a man is, much less how to become one.

If we're going to solve these problems, we'll need to develop a new mind-set. We must not accept the unacceptable as inevitable. Teen rebellion, midlife crisis, and marital meltdown no longer need to be the normal pattern. In one generation, our society can reverse this destructive trend. I am convinced that rites of passage for our young people are the foundation for this reversal.

Now back to my son Christopher: By the time our plane landed in Michigan, I was completely worn out but elated at the results of our trip to Africa. James and I could see our families waving to us from inside the airport as we descended the ramp. Soon we walked into a wonderful welcome of hugs, kisses, and questions from spouses and children.

Later that evening I shared my findings on rites of passage and manhood with Kathleen. As we discussed them in light of our family, we eventually zeroed in on Christopher and his upcoming thirteenth birthday. We soon decided that Christopher would have much more than a standard birthday party to mark his transition into manhood. In less than three weeks, he would have a rite of passage.

CHAPTER 3

PLANNING A MEANINGFUL CELEBRATION

The days following my return from Africa were filled with a flurry of activity. I was two weeks behind in my work and, more important, in time spent with Kathleen, Christopher, Steven, Jenifer, and Daniel. There were letters to write, clients to contact, stories about Africa to be told…and a rite of passage to be created!

Each evening after the children were in bed, Kathy and I would talk about Christopher's upcoming celebration. Our discussions and resulting conclusions were rich with emotion and sometimes painful reflection, especially for me. I often feel that time has become my enemy as I watch my son grow. With each passing day, he becomes more of a man and seems to change before my eyes. I am truly torn by this reality.

As a father, I know I must one day release my son into his own future. Nevertheless, part of me wants to keep him as a little boy forever. I see that his once skinny arms and legs have developed into muscular limbs filled with energy and purpose. The little helper who used to stick by my side during work projects now has other things to do when my tools appear. At times, I long to hear his squeaky voice calling "Daddy" once again. I wish life could be comprised of endless summers spent fishing or playing together. But I also know that if I do not help Christopher continue to grow into a mature man, I run the very real risk of losing him to a lifestyle of childishness that could ultimately destroy him and our relationship. So for this reason, as well as many others, I kept planning for his special day.

One of the most interesting decisions Kathleen and I had to make was what to call our son's event. To call it a *party* made it sound too trite. And the term *ceremony* made it sound as if the attendees would need to dress in flowing saffron robes and chant just to get in the door. We finally settled on the term *celebration* as the most appropriate.

But what would we need to pull together to make it the best kind of celebration for our maturing son? We eventually concluded that two key ingredients were needed: a transmission of wisdom from special mentors and a time of spiritual blessing.

GATHERING THE MENTORS

As we worked to design Christopher's celebration, I was reminded of the people who had invested themselves in my own young life. I wanted to include the best of their wise contributions in the celebration. This was a time of pleasant memories and reflection as I remembered family, friends, and mentors who had encouraged my own growth into manhood…

My mother was always loving and kind, even when my older

brother, younger sister, and I were less than deserving of her gentleness. Her love taught me to care for others.

My dad showed me how to work and taught me never to complain about the hardships of life. I always felt so special when he let me help with one of his "grown-up" projects. He also instilled in me that the Golden Rule would never let me down, and that if I couldn't say something nice, I shouldn't say anything at all.

My beloved Grandpa Henry taught me to hunt, fish, and build things out of wood.

Grandma Alice was the one who spent hours playing on the floor beside me, creating within me a vivid imagination.

My stern but loving *Great-aunt Virginia* instilled in me a desire to excel in my schoolwork and never to accept less than my own best efforts.

A pep talk from *Roger Little,* my junior high basketball coach, gave me the confidence to push my physical skills as far as possible. As a result, I became captain and most valuable player of my Class-A high school team and went on to play basketball in college.

A high school biology teacher, *Fred Case,* taught me to search out the wonders of this world through books. He made it fun to learn.

These fine men and women shaped my character during the first decade and a half of my life. Each provided crucial foundations for my own transition into manhood. Each gave time, love, coaching, instruction, and words of encouragement to a boy searching for the proper way to go in life. Although none of my mentors instituted a rite of passage for me, I knew I could rely on aspects of the love and support they had given me to help design the celebration for Christopher.

Developing the Time of Blessing

Without question, Kathleen and I wanted the celebration to have a strong spiritual foundation. Early in the planning stage, I discovered two biblical accounts of blessing and celebration that really touched me. They gave me a good idea of what to include in our time of blessing.

A Patriarch's Love: Confirming a Son's Identity

The first story revolves around the Hebrew patriarch Jacob (see Genesis 47–49). When old and bent Jacob realizes that his time on earth is nearly over, he calls for his sons so he can see them one last time and bless them before he passes on. A third generation becomes involved in the blessing when Joseph, one of Jacob's sons, arrives with his two young sons, Ephraim and Manasseh.

Jacob's eyesight is very poor, so he only vaguely sees the two grandsons and asks Joseph: "Who are these?" Joseph's response speaks volumes to both his father and his two sons: "These are the sons that God has given me."

Abundant meaning resides in his simple statement! There was no confusion in the boys' minds about their origins. Nor are they left to wonder if they were the result of some random, cosmic mistake. Joseph's words clearly affirm whose family these boys belong to. "These are the sons that *God* has given *me.*"

Jacob's reaction is just as powerful. He immediately tells Joseph to bring the boys close to him so he can bless them. Jacob rises slowly, painfully, to greet them. Countless days in the desert have taken their toll on his body. His beard and hair are no doubt as white as the frost on the high mountains. His cheeks must feel like aged leather, wrinkled and yet soft to the touch. I imagine hands of iron gripping the boys' arms and pulling them close. The boys are in awe of these hands. They surely remembered the stories their father had told them: Grandpa's hands had wrestled with God!

But today they will be hands of blessing. Jacob pulls his grandsons to his chest, where he embraces and kisses them.

I wonder what Ephraim and Manasseh thought as they quietly accepted such a special blessing. Here they are in the presence of their father and grandfather, the two most beloved men in their lives. They realize their grandfather is about to die. Yet, with an infinite number of other things he could have done with his final moments on earth, *he has chosen to bless them.*

Jacob's eyes are failing, but as the boys look deep within them, they catch the reflection of forty thousand sunsets. They feel awkward. Uncertain. *What will he say about us, this man who speaks with God?* they must wonder.

The boys don't have to wait long for the answer. It is time for their rite of passage and blessing. In the presence of their father, Jacob places his hands on the boys' heads and says (in Genesis 48:15-16):

> May the God before whom my fathers
> > Abraham and Isaac walked,
> the God who has been my shepherd
> > all my life to this day,
> the Angel who has delivered me from all harm
> > —may he bless these boys.
> May they be called by my name
> > and the names of my fathers Abraham and Isaac,

and may they increase greatly
        upon the earth.

The boys are enveloped in a cloud of wonder. A surge of excitement courses through their bodies as they realize that their grandfather's sad passing means a new beginning for them. With a glance at their father, they slowly move away from Jacob's side and sit quietly by the foot of his bed.

Outside they can likely hear the footsteps of their uncles, who have come to be blessed as well. Ruben, Judah, and the rest have gathered to see their father one last time before he experiences his own rite of passage into eternity. At Jacob's call, the uncles enter and receive their blessings. Jacob's words are carefully chosen, and he blesses each son with what is appropriate for him.

Jacob then gives instructions concerning his burial. As soon as he finishes, he draws his feet up on his bed and breathes his last.

How powerful that time must have been for everyone involved, especially for the young boys! During their grandfather Jacob's final moments, they experienced spiritual awareness, family relationships, rites of passage, and a sense of purpose that they will carry on their journey to maturity.

Although I was not yet sure how to accomplish it, I wanted my own son to experience something similar, something just as memorable and powerful.

A Son Beloved: Pronouncing a Father's Pleasure

The second biblical account of a father's blessing that impressed me comes in Matthew 3:16-17. It records the events that took place when

Jesus was baptized in the River Jordan and the Holy Spirit descended on him. As Jesus rose out of the water, his Father declared from heaven, "This is my Son, whom I love; with him I am well pleased." Later it is recorded that on the Mount of Transfiguration, the heavenly Father once again said, "This is my Son, whom I love; with him I am well pleased" (Matthew 17:5).

How significant that the Father said, "*This* is my Son." If Jesus in his humanity doubted his divine heritage for even a moment, these few words confirming his Sonship would have put any of those doubts to rest. However, if this was his Father's only purpose, he would have said, "*You* are my beloved Son," addressing Jesus alone. By saying "*This* is my Son," the heavenly Father served notice to all creation that the promised divine Savior had arrived. He let every being in the universe know who this young man was and how his Father felt about him.

Ironically, or perhaps predictably, in just a short time after this wonderful blessing is bestowed, this beloved Son is assaulted by the assorted schemes of Satan. In Matthew 4:1-11, we see the devil tempt Jesus to turn stones into bread, to test the Father's love by casting himself down from a high tower, and to accept all the world's riches if he will turn from his Father and worship the deceiver. Jesus, however, rejects all three temptations, realizing they are but smoke screens for Satan's real objective: to separate Jesus from the blessing, purpose, and identity that his Father had recently bestowed on him. This is why Satan begins two of his seductive statements to Jesus with the words, "*If* you are the Son of God."

If Satan had managed to confuse Jesus about his true identity or convince him that he was not the Son of God, then the course of human history would have been dramatically altered. Instead, Jesus believed his Father, received his identity, and dutifully carried out his heaven-sent mission on earth.

Pressing Ahead

After studying these Bible passages, I was convinced that our celebration needed to include conferring of a blessing, confirmation of Christopher's identity, and a declaration of just how pleased I was with him as my son.

At this point, a vague picture of what our celebration would look like began to emerge. But I was beginning to feel pressed for time. I quietly questioned whether we could create a proper rite of passage within a few short weeks.

In fact, as the preparations continued, a war began to rage within me. Often my mind made weak attempts to minimize the importance of the celebration, only to be overridden by a still small voice in my soul that whispered: *This celebration will change more than one life in some very profound ways.* In less than twenty-one days, I would understand what these words meant.

CHAPTER 4

FINAL PREPARATIONS

Kathleen and I decided we wanted the celebration to be a surprise for Christopher. Looking back, I don't think it would have taken anything away from the evening's impact if our son had known all about the event. But keeping it a secret was part of the fun for us. We learned quickly, though, how difficult it is to keep something secret from an inquisitive, nearly thirteen-year-old boy!

During the early planning stages, we had some basics to arrange. First, we located a medium-sized conference room in a nearby hotel. We considered having the celebration at home or at our church, but for us the hotel seemed like the best choice. We wanted to avoid distractions, even from well-meaning people. Of course, a wide variety of settings would work for this type of celebration, including a wilderness cabin, campgrounds, a private home, a church building, or any available meeting hall. Many of the men who attended Christopher's celebration have since held rites of passage for their own sons in various settings with equal effectiveness.

Next came the arrangements for food and beverages. We wanted the focus to be on the ceremony itself rather than on a dinner, so we chose to provide a cake, coffee, and soft drinks. This was easy to arrange, and it created a casual atmosphere of fellowship at the beginning of Christopher's special night.

Kathleen agreed to take care of these matters, allowing me to concentrate on developing the agenda for the celebration. Since I had no specific pattern to go by, I struggled with where to begin. However, slowly and prayerfully, an outline for the evening began developing in my mind.

A Communication of Value—from Men

I knew that one very significant part of the celebration would occur when godly men communicated to Christopher something of great value from their lives. So I sent the following letter to a select group of men whose lives had demonstrated the qualities I wanted to see in my son.

Dear ———,

Greetings in the name of the Lord!
After prayerful consideration, I am writing to ask you and several other men to help with an event that is most dear to me. My son, Christopher Brian Molitor, is turning thirteen this month, and I believe that we need to celebrate his coming into the first stages of manhood in a special way. I am organizing a gathering of godly men who will pray and speak words of encouragement over my son at a "graduation" ceremony to be held on July 28th. I am requesting that you help in this celebration in some or all of the following ways:

Write a letter to Christopher that addresses growing into mature manhood and includes a selected passage of Scripture, a life lesson that you have personally learned, and a word of blessing. This is the most important aspect of the ceremony, as Chris will treasure these letters as he grows.

Commit to pray for Christopher during this time, asking that God will reveal his perfect plan for him.

Provide a small gift that is symbolic or has particular meaning for a young man growing up. This may be a book, something made by hand, an old fishing lure, a plaque or picture, etc. Please understand that the emphasis here is on the symbolic meaning, not on the gift itself.

Attend the ceremony if you are able. It will be held on Monday, the 28th, at the ———— hotel in Midland from 7 to 10 P.M. Cake, soft drinks, and coffee will be served at the gathering.

Other options: God may give you another idea of how to bless this fine young man. Please feel free to be creative.

I realize that the 28th is drawing close, and I am giving you short notice. Please forgive me for this. If you cannot attend, you may send your letters and/or packages to me at my home. This celebration gathering will be a surprise for my son, so please send your correspondence addressed to me, personally. If your schedule will not permit a mailing, then perhaps you can e-mail your letter and I will print it out for Christopher.

I am indebted to you for your kindness. If I can return the favor for a special young person in your life, just say the

word and I will respond. I want to thank you in advance
for helping me to send this fine young man into God's plan
for his life! Any questions, please call me.

Brian D. Molitor

Despite the fact that these busy men had less than three weeks to prepare, their response to my letter was overwhelming! Businessmen, ministers, and friends from near and far wrote back with their support. That was when the real fun began. It became increasingly difficult to keep the celebration a secret from Christopher. As the letters and packages arrived, Chris was usually right there, checking out the mail. On one occasion, a dear friend of mine forgot to put my name on the envelope and instead addressed his letter to Christopher. Naturally, when it arrived, Chris picked up the letter and started walking toward his room with it. My poor son thought I had lost my mind as I dove across the room to snatch the envelope out of his hands just before he opened it.

As the letters arrived, I continued to fill in the actual agenda for the celebration. I sensed that another part of the evening should be some dramatized skits that conveyed foundational life messages. However, I found it difficult to decide which lessons should be the focus of the evening, much less how to present them. After several days of fruitless planning, I did what we often do when we have exhausted our own supply of ideas: I prayed and asked God what to do. When I woke the following day, I had plans for three skits complete with props, such as pop bottles, a hundred pounds of shelled corn, bags of junk food, and tools. These skits would prove to be a highlight of the celebration.

Next, Kathleen and I talked with the hotel personnel to make sure the room was set up properly. We also bought a new tape for the video camera (Kathleen had jokingly said that if I did not videotape the celebration, the hotel would become my new home). I also made plans to pack my small camera so I could take photographs to fill a scrapbook that I would give to Christopher after the celebration was over. Once all these preparations were completed, we just had to wait for the special day…

GRANDFATHER, FATHER, AND SON

Monday, July 28—the night of the celebration finally arrived. Christopher's grandfather, Jim Hayes, offered to take Chris and me out for a birthday dinner, even though Chris's actual birthday was still two days away.

Jim is a wonderful father-in-law. He is a bear of a man with a grip like a vise, despite the fact he had just reached his eightieth birthday. His easy smile and knowledge of home repairs helped me survive my early years as a homeowner. "Grandpa" Hayes was never more than a phone call away when I sheepishly finished a repair project with more pieces than when I began. Our dinner together was the perfect opener to Christopher's special night.

According to plan, Christopher and I met Jim at a local restaurant at five o'clock. As we talked about the day's earlier activities, I thought about how special it was to have three generations of men gathered together. Grandpa Hayes spoke of the relief he felt when he was finally able to sell some property that had been on the market for the past two years. Christopher offered to take him golfing later that summer, and I spent most of the time watching these two enjoy each other's company. At one point Grandpa Hayes asked Christopher if he had any plans for his birthday. Christopher's quiet response was that "nothing special" was planned. I just sat and smiled as I watched his grandfather's eyes twinkle.

SURPRISE, CHRISTOPHER!

We soon finished our dinner and said good-bye to Grandpa Hayes. As we got into our car, I asked with a straight face, "Where should we go now, pal?"

"How about the movies, Dad? There are some cool shows on tonight," he said excitedly. "They start at seven-thirty."

"Okay. But how about if we stop at the hotel first? There's a prayer meeting tonight, and I told the men that I would stop by."

"But Dad, we only have a little time." Christopher looked disappointed. "When you guys get together, it's hard to get you apart. We'll miss the start of the movie!"

"Don't worry, Son. We'll just stop in to say hello, and we'll leave whenever *you* say you want to, okay?"

My son reluctantly agreed. As we pulled into the hotel parking lot, Christopher noticed several cars that belonged to the men from our church.

"Hey Dad, there's Tony's car, and there's Pastor Ron's car and…"

I just nodded my head and silently hoped I'd given everyone enough time to get into the room before we drove up.

We entered the hotel and made our way down the hallway to the room. As we walked through the door, I was thrilled to see so many men had gathered to celebrate my son's special night. There were nearly thirty in all!

From all outward appearances, these men seemed so different from one another. Some were young and others old. Some had black skin, some brown, and others white. Some were wealthy and others had very few material possessions. But their genuine smiles spoke volumes about the glue that held them together: These men all shared a common love for their Maker, for their families, and for their friends.

I liked these men. They weren't handwringers who chose to huddle together to complain about the unfairness or troubles of their lives. Rather, these were gentle warriors from all walks of life who had chosen to stand for what is eternally good. They were men who came together to share the common load of life and to bear each other's burdens. Men who did their best to live out their commitment to truth. Their presence at my son's special night filled me with a renewed appreciation for the gift of friendship. My only regret is that I failed to get a photograph of Christopher's face when he first saw all those wonderful men in the room. It took a while for him to realize that this gathering was being held in his honor.

Seated in the far corner of the room was a grinning Grandpa Hayes, who had driven from the restaurant in record time and had arrived just before we walked in. Three of the men had brought their teenage sons—Caleb, Nick, and Patrick—to participate in the celebration, as well. Christopher quickly gravitated to them.

I hustled around the room, making last-second changes in the seating arrangements, setting up the video camera, and putting the props in position for the skits. The room was ideal for our needs. We had a large area of comfortable chairs where the men sat and talked, and there was also a formal area with tables, chairs, and a podium arranged so that everyone would have a good view of the presentations and skits.

It was obvious that my precious wife had been in the room earlier in the day. Colorful decorations brightened the walls. Kathy had also brought a large sheet cake that was displayed on a table by the entryway. At her instructions, the bakery had written a Scripture verse on the white frosting: "When I was a child, I talked like a child, I thought like a child, I reasoned like a child. When I became a man, I put childish ways behind me" (1 Corinthians 13:11). How appropriate those words! They brought tears to my eyes. Truly this was going to be a rite of passage for my son. I silently thanked God for his grace.

After an opening prayer, we cut the cake and enjoyed refreshments and fellowship for the next half-hour. I marveled at the fact that so many men had gathered to bless my son. Their laughter was genuine, their sharing heartfelt. A subtle fragrance and a sense of peace filled the room that night.

It was easy for me to picture Jesus' first disciples meeting like this. I could almost hear the soft steps of the Master as he moved among us. His words rose up in my memory: "For where two or three are gathered together in My name, I am there in the midst of them" (Matthew 18:20, NKJV). Later that evening, he made his presence known to us in ways we'd never anticipated.

CHAPTER 5

LESSONS FOR LIFE

After we finished our refreshments, the group gathered for the start of the formal ceremony. Christopher and his friends sat toward the front of the room, where they would have a clear view of the proceedings.

I opened by thanking the men for coming. As I looked into their faces, I was flooded with fond memories. I saw my friend Charlie and thought of the time we'd hunted elk together in the mountains of Colorado. My eyes fell on my dear Christian brother and coworker, James Glenn. The two of us had enjoyed even a deeper bond of friendship since our trip to South Africa. Then I caught the ready smile of Richard, my partner in a small company that I helped him start the previous year. My faithful pastor, Ron Ives, sat in the back of the room, his eyes already moist from the powerful sense of purpose we all felt just by being there.

I then moved ahead with the program, explaining to Christopher that some of the men had volunteered to help with several skits. This announcement brought laughter from the "volunteers." They vocalized mock protests and complained that they didn't recall freely signing up for theatrical assignments.

How Should a Man Deal with His Emotions?

Our first "volunteer," James, walked to the podium and began speaking about the role emotions play in a man's life. He spoke from experience. James grew up on the mean streets of Detroit, Michigan, and had become the man of his house at age eleven when his father abandoned his mother and siblings. James then turned to Christopher and solemnly shared that there were right and wrong ways for men to deal with their emotions.

Then, on cue, another friend, Tony, stormed to the front of the room. In his hand was a large bottle of sparkling carbonated water. Taped to the bottle was a sign that read MY LIFE. Tony began complaining loudly about some of life's problems. Christopher's young eyes spread wide as Tony's tirade grew louder and angrier.

"Man, my wife sure makes me mad!" Tony seethed. "She's always making me jealous! She does it on purpose, too!" His anger seemed intensely real. With each harsh statement, he slammed the soda-water bottle into the palm of his powerful hand.

"My boss is such a jerk! Who does she think she is? I work like a dog and she promotes somebody else!" His face reddened. "I should have gotten that job. It's not fair!" *Bang!* went the carbonated-water bottle as it crashed onto the tabletop in front of Christopher's face. His young eyes were riveted on Tony as the tantrum escalated.

"How am I ever going to get through this?" Tony said in a now fearful tone. "I could lose *everything* if it doesn't get better." He seemed genuinely scared as he complained about his frustrations and gave voice to his fears. And he kept shaking, slamming, and even dropping the fizzing bottle throughout the performance.

Then Tony's demeanor changed. His voice calmed, and he began reflecting on his faith in God.

"Despite all my troubles, I am a Christian, and I want to pour out my life for others. That is what God expects."

With that, Tony made his way to the table where three empty glasses sat. These represented the lives of other people. As he began to twist the top off the bottle, we could all see the words MY LIFE inscribed on its side.

When the top of the bottle was removed, all of the pressure that had built up during the angry tirade was released in a shower of liquid. Those in the front of the room dove for cover. Tony was instantly drenched from his head to his waist. Without a word, he tried to pour what was left of the bottle's contents into the three empty glasses. Sadly, there was only enough left to cover the bottom of each glass. Even the paper sign on the bottle spoke volumes. It hung in soggy tatters, the ink running down the side of the bottle. Tony's "life" was truly a mess!

The room remained silent as our wet friend made his way out into the hall. Then James returned to the podium and solemnly asked us to ponder our own lives. How do we, as men, handle our emotions? How much of our life is left to pour into others after we've devastated it with excess rage or futile flailing? Do our out-of-control emotions rob those around us of a blessing?

Suddenly, Tony re-entered the room wearing a dry shirt. In his hands was another bottle of sparkling water with another MY LIFE label on the front. He had the same angry look on his face as he began to repeat the complaints about his wife we'd heard minutes earlier. He hissed through clenched teeth about the jealousy that tormented his soul.

As he finished venting this time, he again raised the bottle to slam it down into his fist. At the last second, though, he gently placed the bottle on the table and fell to his knees. He poured his heart out to God. "Dear Lord, please help me deal with this jealousy." The passion in his voice was real. "It's eating me alive, and I cannot overcome it on my own. God, please help me."

Tony then rose to his feet, picked up the bottle, and put his "life" back in his own hands. His countenance changed again as another tirade of angry words spilled out. "Man, my boss is so unfair!" he raged. "Why didn't she pick me for the promotion? It just isn't fair!" Again, the bottle was raised above his head. Would he slam it down again? No. Instead, he gently placed it back on the table and walked slowly over to James.

"James, I'm really hurting. Will you pray for me?"

The two of them took each other's hands and prayed together. Tony looked relieved as they finished praying. One last time, Tony picked up the bottle and spoke. "There's too much happening today. I don't know how I'm going to make it."

The men in the room could easily relate to those feelings.

"It's just too much to take sometimes!" Once more, the bottle seemed headed for a blow that would cause it to erupt when opened. But Tony surprised us again. He gently set the bottle down and walked humbly towards Pastor Ron. His words were simple and quiet. "Brother, I need some help."

Many of us in the room were moved to tears as Pastor Ron simply hugged Tony. No words needed to be spoken. The moment was filled with power as God used one man to strengthen another. Then Tony picked up the bottle and made his way to the three glasses.

"I know that God wants me to pour my life into others," he said quietly as he twisted the cap on the bottle. Instinctively, those nearest the bottle started to pull back. Would it explode as the first one had? When the top was removed, there was barely a sound. Not a drop was spilled. We all watched in wonder as one man symbolically poured his life into the lives of others. Amazingly, each glass was filled exactly to the top as the final drop fell from Tony's bottle.

The men there had witnessed a critical life lesson: When we deal with our emotions properly, not only do our own lives flow much better, but we have plenty to pour into our families and the other people who God places in our path.

Tony carefully set his now-empty bottle down on the table. This time, the sign on the side of the bottle spoke an entirely different message. The ink was dry. The sign was intact. One life had been emptied so that three others could be filled.

Christopher sat stunned, his young face filled with awe at the power of the message. In fifteen minutes, he had learned more about how men should deal with their emotions than many men learn in a lifetime.

But the lessons were just beginning.

DOES A REAL MAN HAVE TO GO IT ALONE?

Doug, a big man with salt-and-pepper hair, walked deliberately toward the front of the room. A devoted husband and father, Doug also serves as an elder in our local church. His burly frame projects physical strength, while his kind and gentle manner reflects the love of the Father.

"Christopher," he called out in his soothing baritone voice. "Please come up here."

After the exploding bottle in the last skit, my son looked a little hesitant to comply. Cautiously, he left his seat and stood next to Doug.

"Chris, I have a job for you to do."

"Okay. What is it?"

"Just carry a couple of things to the back of the room."

"Sure, what are they?"

Doug stepped aside to reveal two fifty-pound bags of shelled corn I had purchased from a feed store earlier in the week. Christopher's muscles bulged as he labored to pick up the first bag. He is a strong young man, but the bag of corn was like many situations in a man's life: It was hard to get a handle on! When Chris picked up one end of the bag, all of the weight shifted into the other end, and he nearly toppled over. He finally got the first bag balanced and started lugging it toward the back of the room.

After he had walked several yards, Doug asked him to stop. "Chris, how are you coming with that burden you're carrying? Is the job easy or difficult?"

Christopher responded with a typical male answer: "Well, it isn't easy, but I know I can do it." Doug's comeback captured both sides of a man's approach to handling the burdens in his life.

"Chris, it's great that you tried," Doug said kindly. "I can see that you're not afraid to work, nor are you a complainer. But since you have another bag to move, let's just take a moment to pray. Let's ask God to show you someone in the room who might come and help you."

Chris seemed relieved by the suggestion. He immediately set the bag down, bowed his head, and earnestly prayed. "Dear Jesus, please show me who should come help me with this task. Thank you, Lord. Amen."

As his eyes opened, he immediately said three names: "Caleb, Nick, and Tony." The three quickly jumped out of their seats and moved toward the bags. Chris and Caleb took the first one, and the other two grabbed the second bag. In short order, the task was completed, and everyone returned to his seat.

While the lesson was intended for Christopher, everyone in the room could easily see the natural tendency in men to want to go it alone. We seem to think we can always handle life by ourselves, no matter what comes along.

Doug then began a short teaching on the need to have friends we can count on to share our burdens and lend the support we need. He shared that men often become like solitary bull elephants. These majestic creatures are clearly in charge of their domain, but they manage it from the edges. They protect their herd and only interact with others in their families and communities when absolutely necessary. No one dares challenge these silent leaders. And no one dares try to help them either. The loners' dominance lasts until they face enemies or obstacles they cannot overcome alone. Inevitably, each one will face a situation that he can't overcome by himself. Then he will fall.

The nodding heads around the room showed that Doug's points were well made and accepted. We all need others to help us through life's challenges. Truly, as it says in Ecclesiastes 4:12, a cord of three strands is not easily broken.

Doug then added an interesting twist to the skit. He questioned the three helpers about how they felt when asked to assist with the task. One by one, they responded.

"Honored."

"Chosen."

"I felt needed."

"Did anyone feel put out or upset when you had to leave the comfort of your chairs in order to help Chris?" asked Doug.

After a few seconds, Caleb spoke up. "Jesus is our role model. He came to serve, not to be served. Sometimes we forget that. There's no way I could just sit here and watch my friend struggle with the load. Man, I wanted to help!"

Next, Doug shared how men often get into tough situations and, instead of asking God to show them the way out, they try working harder on their own. Many heads dropped. We could all relate. God said his ways are higher than our ways and his thoughts higher than our thoughts (Isaiah 55:8-9), so why are we so stubborn sometimes? God always provides a way out for us, no matter what form of temptation comes our way (see 1 Corinthians 10:13). But to find God's way out, we need to ask him for the solution and then be willing to let others help us.

It was now becoming obvious that the lessons shared during the celebration were intended for more than just a thirteen-year-old. The Lord had prepared a delicious meal filled with some of life's greatest lessons, and he was inviting each one of us to dine.

As I looked at the smiles on the men's faces and reflected on what had happened already, it was hard to imagine that there was more to come. But as Pastor Ron walked to the podium, I soon learned that when the Lord prepares the meal, it truly is a feast!

WHAT KINDS OF CHOICES WILL YOU MAKE, KID?

"A man must make many choices in his life," said Pastor Ron. "Right choices make for a good life, wrong choices make for a bad life. It is just that simple."

Clearly, Pastor Ron knew what he was talking about. He is a successful father, husband, and pastor, loved deeply by his family and his congregation. He had made some great choices along life's way. But one thing I like about this man is his willingness to share with others about a few of the wrong choices he made early in life. The subtle lines at the corners of his eyes gave silent testimony to a period of hard living and bad choices.

"Christopher, I want you to go shopping," Pastor encouraged. "Please come up to the front."

On the table at the front of the room were several items "for sale." And what an assortment! The items were arranged in two opposing piles. On the left side of the table were a bottle of whiskey, a fake pornographic magazine, some junk food, and a few children's toys. On the right side were a bottle of pure spring water, a Bible, a loaf of fresh-baked whole wheat bread, and a new hammer.

Christopher's face reflected a blend of joy and apprehension. As he started forward, so did two other men. Each "salesman" moved behind one set of items and waited for his turn to try to sell his wares to Christopher.

Chuck, a wildly animated guy, began his sales pitch for the worldly items. "Hey kid!" he hollered as he reached out to grab Christopher's shirt. "Come here. I've got everything you need for this life. Check out this magazine, man. Look at these women. These are the real thing! This kind of stuff will make you a man!"

When Chris showed no interest in the magazine, Chuck's tactics changed, and he grabbed the bottle of whiskey. "Look kid, you're too uptight tonight. You need to loosen up a bit," he said. "Let's have a few drinks and then things will look better. Eat, drink, and be merry, that's what the Bible says, right?"

"Ah, no thanks…," said Christopher quietly.

"Okay, no problem," interrupted Chuck. "I can see you're a growing boy, so how about some chow? I got some great stuff here. Lots of fat and sugar. Plenty of special dyes to give these goodies a nice orange color." Chuck literally shoved the bag of junk food into Chris's face. "Let's eat!"

"I don't think so," said Chris as he pulled away from the salesman's impassioned pleas. Chuck began to sound desperate as he noticed Christopher's attention shifting to the quiet man standing behind the other group of items for sale. "Listen kid, I know what you're thinking. It's time to grow up, right? Take it from me, there is always time for that—later. Here, grab some of these toys. You sure don't want to learn about work, do you? It's time to play, so let's play! The Bible says you're supposed to play like a little child, right? Hey, come on. Where are you going?"

"I'm going to look over here," Chris answered as he turned toward the other salesman who stood quietly with his hands folded in front of him.

But Chuck wasn't going to take "no" for an answer.

"Wait a minute! Don't be stupid!" he screamed as his smile turned into a snarl. Picking up the porn magazine, he began his hard sell. "Blondes, brunettes, redheads! All *real* men love this stuff! Hey, what's the hurry? Come on, just stay with me for a little while. Couple of drinks can't hurt, can they? What's the hurry? Hey, no money down. I'll collect from you later…"

Many of us in the room laughed at Chuck's antics as he tried in vain to hook the young man into staying. Yet behind our laughter, we remembered the many times we'd succumbed to the seductive call of bad choices and temporary pleasures. We were reminded that the Scriptures are to be prayerfully studied, not swallowed in simple sound bites nor twisted, as Chuck was doing. We each carried the physical and emotional scars to prove the destructive impact of stopping and shopping at the wrong places.

Choices. What did Pastor Ron say? "Right choices make for a good life, wrong choices make for a bad life. It is just that simple."

The next salesman was Pastor Gary. His gentle demeanor and strong faith made him an excellent representative for his products from "Kingdom of God Enterprises."

"Son," he began softly. "Those things at the other end of the table may look or sound good, and they might be pretty exciting, at first. But there is one major problem with them: They don't satisfy."

Those last three words hit the rest of us hard. *They don't satisfy.* So many of us had learned that the hard way. Pastor Gary continued. "The problem is that you have to keep going back for more and more of that junk. I'll bet the salesman didn't tell you that, did he?"

Chris thought for a moment and acknowledged that Chuck had not.

Holding up the Bible, Gary began his heavenly sales pitch. "The words in *this* book will never disappoint you, Son. You will never have to hide it or be ashamed of it. If you want to learn about women, this is the book for you. It will teach you how to love and respect them. Women are much more than just body parts. They are created in God's image. But this wonderful book isn't limited to just one subject. This is a handbook for your life!"

His words rolled like gentle thunder across the room. We knew that God was giving us all a reminder to stay with the words of life. We were convicted that there were too many times we ourselves had bypassed the Bible on the way to the television set or our favorite hobby.

"As for his brand of food and drink," Gary smiled and nodded his head toward Chuck. "They will definitely fill you *out,* but in the end they will leave you empty. It's easy to forget that *we* are the temples of the Holy Spirit, not toxic waste dumps. God wants us to put only good things into our bodies. Son, try this bread and spring water. They are not only good for you but will also remind you that Jesus is *the* Bread of Life and his Word washes us like pure water.

"Christopher, you have enjoyed a fine childhood. Your parents have cared for your needs, and you have lacked little as you have grown. You've played for hours with toys like those on the table over there. And yes, Jesus did say that we were to *enter* the kingdom as little children. But he didn't say that we were to spend the rest of our lives there just playing, remaining immature and unproductive. His Word tells us that 'If a man will not work, he shall not eat'" (2 Thessalonians 3:10).

That got my son's attention!

ARE YOU READY TO GET TO WORK?

"As a servant of God and as a man," Gary added, "you will experience many times of enjoyment, fun, and laughter. But these are the results of being in relationship with your heavenly Father and in obedience to his

Word and to his ways. You will learn that there is nothing more enjoyable than being used by the Master to further his kingdom. Also, there are few things in life more satisfying than for a man to build something for and with his family. Christopher, it is time to set aside the toys of childhood and pick up the tools of a man."

Christopher picked up the hammer and stared thoughtfully at it. I imagined him using it to build his dream house some time in the future. In my mind's eye, I saw *his* sons—my grandsons —clinging to his legs as he tried to build. *"Daddy, Daddy," they called out. "Can we help?"*

Then I remembered projects in the past when Christopher and I had worked together. Those first few were especially memorable. I spent more time undoing his messes than working on the project. But I realized that in those times God was doing so much more than building doghouses and go-carts. He was using those times together to teach my son to work like a man and to press forward even when obstacles temporarily blocked the way. To fight the urge to quit in frustration when a nut was rusted tight or a part was missing from a box. God also used those times to bond our hearts together.

In that moment, it became so clear to me that the plan of God is to have one generation of men serve as the teachers, mentors, counselors, and friends to the next generation of men. What a wonderful plan! But how many boys and young men have never had an older man serve them in this way? How many men in the room with me were still hurting, still needing someone to affirm their manhood?

Pastor Ron's voice broke my train of thought.

"Christopher, it's time to make your purchases. You have heard both salesmen. What will you buy?"

I held my breath for a second as my son glanced at the first set of goods. Then he literally turned his back on Chuck and opened his shopping bag for Pastor Gary to fill. In went the Bible, bread, water, and hammer. As my son made his way back to his seat, the men clapped and cheered.

None of us were naive enough to believe that a little skit would prevent Chris from ever listening to the voices of worldly salesmen when he was on his own. However, we felt sure that when he did hear those voices with their seductive promises, he would remember: *I don't have to shop here; I can make good choices.* It is just that simple.

The skit left us feeling full and yet still hungry for more. We were thrilled to think that this fine young man might never have to experience the pain so many of us had suffered from our shopping trips to the wrong places.

It seemed as if I was floating on air as I moved to the podium to announce our next step in the celebration.

CHAPTER 6

LEADERS SHARING
WORDS AND GIFTS

S on, I have some letters here for you," I said to Christopher. "Some are from men whom you know. Others were sent by men you have never met—friends of mine from other countries. These are all special letters. I asked these men to pray before they wrote anything down, and I am sure they did. Christopher, I want you to understand that these men are husbands, fathers, businessmen, clergy, and community leaders. They are very busy men who have no time to waste, yet each took time to seek God for wisdom that they could share with you."

My soon-to-be teenager sat ramrod straight and carefully considered my words. As he looked at the letters in my hand, I could see expectancy in his green eyes. I stole a brief moment for myself as I thought about how my son had changed since the day he entered this world. I was amazed at how many stages he had already passed through. Could this be the chubby-faced little boy who just a few years ago viewed cards and letters as major roadblocks to the fun of opening packages at Christmas or birthdays?

It looked like him, but his face was now different. His cheeks are no longer chubby; instead, they're lean and there is a hint of a mustache on his upper lip. When he was younger, a gathering like this would have intimidated him. He never would have been more than an arm's length away from me. At that age, an invisible cord tied us together. I would always lead and he would always follow. Yet now here he sits in quiet confidence at the head of the table.

For a moment, I feel very proud at his growth. But in the next instant I am chilled by the unthinkable. *Does his growing independence mean that the invisible cord between us is being cut? Am I about to lose my precious son?* No, the cord that binds my son and me will never be severed. But in God's perfect plan, it will lengthen. Just enough for him to experience the joys and sorrows of manhood, but never so much that we lose the special love we have for each other. I could barely contain my emotions.

"This first letter is from a friend of mine in South Africa," I said to Chris. "He is a businessman, husband, father, and former soldier in Rhodesia. Most important, he is a man who honors God with his life, family, and work. After his letter, I'll read several others from people who could not be with us tonight. Then the men who are here have some letters and gifts for you."

I did a fair job of reading the first letter or two. The more I read, however, the harder it was to keep from weeping. The toughest letter to read came from my father, who couldn't attend because he was recovering from a near-fatal heart attack. As I read my dad's letter, I remembered some of the places, times, and events he and I had shared together over the years.

Recalling a Precious Relationship

In my mind's eye, I could see my dad coming home from his job as a superintendent at a General Motors plant in Michigan. My brother, sister, and I would excitedly watch for his car to turn into the driveway at the end of each day.

As I held Dad's letter, my mind flashed back to times spent trout fishing with him on the Pine River in northern Michigan. The opening day of trout season was a very special event in the Molitor family. There was gear to pack, fly lines to be treated (so they'd float just right on the surface of the water), trout flies to tie, waders to patch, and food to prepare.

I recalled that at age five I was certain I was old enough to go with my dad and his father, my beloved Grandpa Henry, when they made the annual pilgrimage to the river. But despite my pleadings and tears, I wasn't allowed to go with them. Not yet. The river was beautiful, but it was also dangerously unforgiving for a small boy who might fall into its swift current.

It seemed as if I would never get to go with my heroes! Upon hearing the bad news, I ran and hurled myself onto my bed for a time of very real sorrow. I hid under my covers, but I was careful to leave one hand exposed—just in case my dad couldn't find me concealed there. Soon I heard Dad's footsteps coming down the hall, and I felt my bed sag under his weight as he sat next to me. Over the years I have forgotten the exact words he spoke to me, yet I remember how he stroked my hair with his strong hand. There was comfort and even a sort of healing in my father's hands. Just that simple touch chased away my pain and reaffirmed his love for me. I realized then that his motive for keeping me home was protection, not rejection. That touch sealed his promise that someday I would go with him.

Two years later my dream came true. Dad was pretty sneaky when it came to surprises. He called me into our living room about one week before that year's opening day. Just by the tone of his voice, I knew he was up to something. When I entered the room, I saw a complete set of fishing gear made just the right size for me. My eyes immediately fell on the most beautiful fly rod I'd ever seen. Its shiny blue finish and intricate gold thread windings spoke volumes to me. I knew that it signified something incredibly important: I had made a transition in my father's eyes.

Several days later we made the long trip to our cabin for my first trout opener. I don't remember if I caught any fish that day, but it really didn't matter. I was with my two heroes—my father and grandpa—and that was enough for a seven-year-old fisherman with a new fly rod.

With these wonderful memories replaying in my mind, I started reading aloud the letter from my dad, while Christopher watched and listened.

Dear Chris,

This is your grandfather writing. The one whom you used to call Grandpa MUTTITOR when you were only two or three years old.

Well, you are about to become a teenager! You are certainly ahead of your father and me, at the same age, regarding your beliefs and knowledge of our Lord. What we had was a general concept of sin, a locker room education regarding girls and sex (never did completely understand girls), and frequent admonitions to "be good." We were just lukewarm Christians well into adulthood. Fortunately, we got there in time.

No one can really prepare you for the teen years. If we told you, you wouldn't believe us regarding all the physical, mental, and emotional changes that will take place. Keep the faith and conscience the Lord has given to you; the Golden Rule rarely lets you down.

Just so there is an equal opportunity flavor to these thoughts, your Grandmother and I share them, and are very proud of a boy named Chris.

Love,

Grandpa Molitor

As I finished reading the letter, I couldn't help thinking about the events that had nearly claimed Dad's life earlier that year and prevented his attendance on this special night. The ordeal began when Kathy and I had received a chilling phone call from my mother at 2 A.M. Dad had suffered a severe heart attack, she told us, and was being rushed by ambulance to the hospital. As I drove the twenty miles into town, I was filled with fear. Dad and I had so much more to say to each other! Was this the end? At that point, only God knew.

The hospital was a blur of foreign sounds and smells. Soon family and friends had assembled there to wait for some word of Dad's condition. I spent much of that time in the hospital chapel with my faithful friend James Glenn. Together, we petitioned our heavenly Father for an outpouring of his grace and mercy.

As the day wore on, a series of bad reports filtered back to us. A cardiac catheterization procedure revealed severe blockages in Dad's heart, leading doctors to rush him to open-heart surgery. Hours passed. Next we were told he was in the recovery room. Then more complications, and Dad was returned to the operating room for a second open-heart surgery. It was more than twelve hours before all the procedures were completed. Finally, Dad was taken to the cardiac intensive care unit of the hospital. For nearly two weeks, he lay unconscious, with only the steady, slow beeping of a heart monitor indicating he was still alive.

Twice each day, my family and I were allowed to see him. He looked so helpless, like a little child. We would gather around his body, praying for God to heal him. One day as I sat on his bed, I realized I had been stroking his hair as he had stroked mine so many years earlier. Thankfully, two weeks later, our prayers were answered, and he was released from the hospital to finish his recuperation at home.

On Christopher's special day, Dad was still recovering, and my precious mom was serving as his nurse. I knew Dad was praying for Christopher, and it was fun to think that someday the two of them might fish for trout together. I soon finished reading his letter and returned to my chair. Next, it was time to have the men in the room come forward to share their letters with Christopher.

Hearing from Men's Hearts

Each letter was unique. Each brought a slightly different perspective on manhood and the journey to maturity. When combined, the letters served as modern-day commentaries on key scriptures and a handbook for any man's life and conduct.

One by one, my friends came to the front of the room to share words written on paper, revealing the wisdom hidden in their hearts. Pastor Ron was the first to read his letter:

Chris,

What an honor it is for me to be a part of this graduation! I have enjoyed watching you mature into a young man. Challenges undoubtedly await you, but the deposit of God within you is more than able to face all of them.

Chris, a portion of Scripture that I have memorized and would consider a "life verse" for me in regards to goals and motivation would be Philippians 3:7-11…

"But whatever was to my profit I now consider loss for the sake of Christ. What is more, I consider everything a loss compared to the surpassing greatness of knowing Christ Jesus my Lord, for whose sake I have lost all things. I consider them rubbish, that I may gain Christ and be found in him, not having a righteousness of my own that comes from the law, but that which is through faith in Christ—the righteousness that comes from God and is by faith. I want to know Christ and the power of his resurrection and the fellowship of sharing in his sufferings, becoming like him in his death, and so, somehow, to attain to the resurrection from the dead."

A closing word of encouragement from me would be to develop friendships with your brothers in Christ. Chris, words cannot express the impact these types of relationships

*have had on my life. There have been times that just seeing
another brother has imparted courage into me to press on.*

*Chris, I bless you in the name of the Lord Jesus Christ.
May God's Word dwell in you richly and release life. May
communion with the Holy Spirit encourage and comfort
you. May the Father's love cause you to walk in courage and
strength.*

*I am proud of you as a young man. I am very blessed to
have you as a friend and as a friend of my son.*

Pastor Ron

When he finished reading, Ron carefully handed the letter to Christopher and returned to his seat.

John Paige then made his way to the podium. John is a high-level corporate executive for a multinational company. Through men like him, Christopher saw examples of how God works both inside and outside of a church building.

Dear Chris,

*I thought I would share with you what I have learned about
being a "strong" man of God. The godly picture of strength is
seen in how Jesus lived when He was on earth.... The picture
of Jesus is one of a Man who is physically strong, possessing
wisdom, and gentle with those weaker or less fortunate. Jesus
was filled with God's wisdom and gentle strength.*

Jesus is the perfect role model for a young man like

yourself. Also understand that God doesn't expect you to become perfect on your thirteenth birthday either. What God desires from you and each of us is steady growth. Turn to God for direction in everything you do in life, and He will guide you.

John Paige
2 Timothy 2:22-26

Next, it was Grandpa Hayes's turn to share his letter, which he asked me to read to Christopher. How special to hear the words of a man in his eighties! As I read, others in the room were studying the older man and the boy's reaction to his counsel. The men seemed to understand that each wrinkle in Grandpa's skin represented more than just age. Wisdom, experience, pain, victories, and suffering—all were found in the lines on his face and in the lines of his letter. Many of us shed tears as we heard what he had to say.

Dear Christopher,

I feel real honored to attend this very special occasion this evening in your honor. There have never been two grand-parents that could be more proud and could love their grandchildren more than your grandmother and me. The Lord has really blessed us by sparing us for these many years to enjoy our little family. And we are hoping and praying that He may give us a few more good years.

The Lord has really blessed us with such a wonderful

family. To begin with, you have been blessed with two won-
derful parents and siblings, and you're being raised in a
good Christian home. There are so many children today that
aren't that fortunate.

There are so many more opportunities out there today
than when we were growing up. I gave four years of my life
in the navy to fight for my country and to make it a better
world, and other than that it was just a lot of hard work to
make a good living for my family. So my advice to you,
Chris, is to get a good education, which I'm sure you will...

I have a little sentimental token here, Chris—a
Christmas tree ornament—which was given to us by your
mom and dad during the Christmas holidays in 1983. It
was their way of letting us know they were expecting their
first child. So your mom and grandmother shed a few tears
together. We were all so happy. I am passing it on to you so
that maybe someday, when you have a family of your own,
you may use it on your own Christmas tree. May it always
remind you of your grandma and me.

Chris, you have been such a joy to us over the past thir-
teen years. You are a very special grandson. If you ever need
advice for anything, feel free to come to me, at any time.
But I'm sure your mom and dad will do a good job. I know
you'll grow up to be a fine young man.

We love you dearly.

With all my love,
Grandpa Hayes—age 80

After Grandpa Hayes's letter was read, the other men came forward to share their thoughts with Christopher. Each letter was powerful and touching. Here are some excerpts:

First, I want to encourage you to begin to understand the special heritage you have in your family. God provided for a special dynamic to be possible within the family that cannot be found in any other social structure. Always remember, no matter where you are or what you are going through, whether good or bad, you must never hesitate to receive the love and comfort available to you through your family.

Next, understand that God has given you a dad who is special. I have the opportunity to meet hundreds of people as I travel around the world regularly. Please believe me when I tell you that there are very few men of his caliber in the world today. Having stated this, you must discover and take advantage of what God has in mind for you, in providing such a special man to be your father. You can always count on godly wisdom when you seek advice from your dad because he will always have your best interest in his heart. Nothing or no one should ever become more important in your life than your relationship with God.

The teenage years are some of the hardest years to serve God. One of the reasons is that there is a lot of temptation. It is very easy to stray away from God; however, I have no doubt that you will make it. One important thing is to stay faithful in having quiet times for prayer and Bible reading. I have struggled in this and I have noticed that when I struggled with my quiet times, I also struggled in my walk with God. So stay strong in God and you will have no problem with fending off peer pressure.

My simple word of advice, of encouragement, is to be strong, be courageous, and be of good cheer because the Lord will always be near.

Throughout the course of your life, I'm sure that you will encounter times that your faith in Jesus will be tested, times that you will stand in the face of mighty mountains and some not so mighty but still mountains. Those are the times that I want you to think of that tiny little mustard seed that Jesus spoke of. As small as the mustard seed is, Jesus said, if we have even that much faith, "nothing will be impossible for you."

Chris, if most men could live their lives over, they would want to begin where you are today. We know it's at the entryway of manhood that one's vision of the future begins to take shape.

Childhood is great, but maturity is even better. As a child you have received great blessing from those around you. Certainly you have had opportunities to give and bless others also. As you mature, you will have increasing opportunities to give of your life, time, talents, spiritual gifts, money, etc....I strongly encourage you to give with the express purpose of encouragement and evangelism. "Live to give" always in the light of eternity.

"He is no fool who gives that which he can't keep in order to gain that which he can't lose." (Missionary Jim Elliott)

A man of God once gave me this phrase to consider: "Plant a thought and you will reap an action; plant an action and you will reap a habit; plant a habit and you will reap a lifestyle; plant a lifestyle and you will reap a destiny." I smiled and nodded my acceptance of the ideas he had expressed—but didn't take them too seriously. But later, as I pondered what his words meant, the Lord began to show me how thoughts are the building blocks that will shape our destinies. Our thoughts are the powerful "first steps" which deserve serious and prayerful discrimination.

I see you as a fine young man with a heart for God who, if given the right guidance, has a potential of becoming a great leader in the body of Christ. I am excited to be a small part in facilitating your growth as a man of God.

Now at the coming of age, this first stage of manhood, my advice and plea to you is LISTEN TO YOUR PARENTS.

By listening and being obedient, you will avoid a lot of difficulties in life. One of the Ten commandments, #5, says (Exodus 20:12, KJV), "Honor thy father and thy mother: that thy days may be long upon the land which the LORD thy God giveth thee." This commandment ends with a promise (see Ephesians 6:2). I had no one to tell me these things, but now I am relating them to you. Learn this now at your beginning of manhood, and you will be on the right path.

In the short time I have known you, Christopher, I have appreciated your love for the Lord and your quiet, respectful demeanor. At a time when many young men become mouthy and unrestrained, you have been a tremendous example for my son. Thank you.

There is only one sure way to be smart and flexible, to know when to hang loose and when to bite the bullet. There is only one way to be tough and kind, there is only one way to be focused and yet have peripheral vision. It is the way I am still learning, an art I have yet to master. It is always, in everything, in every decision, in every word to be led by the Holy Ghost. I pray God's strength and patience for you as you learn this art of walking in the Spirit.

During this time, while so much attention is coming your way, my strongest encouragement to you is to always put others first, especially those closest to you. Whether you like it or not, you are a leader, especially to your brothers and sister,

even though you may feel as if they don't respect you at times.
You have, and always will have, great influence on them.

Chris, I want you to know that I have tremendous respect
for you as a godly young man. I know that this transition
into manhood will bring with it even more respect as well as
wisdom and maturity. Your future looks very bright, and
there is only one thing that can dim it, and that's you!
Remember, the best leaders always lead by making right
decisions so they can lead by their successes, not failures. God
has fully equipped you for success!

As I watched the last man leave the podium, it struck me that these men were the living epistles Scripture speaks about. Imperfect men in an imperfect world being led by a perfect God. Each of their letters was a mini-sermon on life for any man. They told of lessons learned in the fires and floods of life. Some, with neither complaint nor excuse, told of the pain felt when a man loses his way. And yet, unlike many of the world's writers who lament life's problems and leave readers in despair, these men pointed the way to the answers. Each man offered hope and a future to a much younger man whose life was filled with so much promise. And many of the men, along with their letters, offered Chris other expressions of their care and concern for him.

Receiving Some Powerful Gifts

Grandpa Molitor had sent along something quite special. It was a long-blade knife he had used as a Boy Scout in 1937. I remember watching my dad fillet rainbow trout with that knife when I was Christopher's age. The knife's blade was no longer shiny, and its sheath was weathered, but it was a treasure nonetheless. Later, I told Christopher about the good memories that knife brought whenever I saw it.

One man gave Chris a beautiful woodsman's compass, and another gave him a road map. Each of these men spoke in parables about God's direction for a young man.

Others gave plaques, candles, music tapes, and CDs. A unique gift from a mountain climber in the group was a metal link used to safely traverse mountain slopes. On it was the inscription, "Jesus is your link to life." Another man took the time to make a videotape of his "letter" so Chris could replay it at home. It included a song about manhood from a popular Christian music group.

James Glenn gave Christopher a beautiful silver nugget ring with a dove etched into the metal. It had been one of his prized possessions for over fifteen years, yet he gladly gave it to Christopher on this special night.

The list goes on. A Bible, a concordance, several books about manhood, a 1984 coin set, posters of Chris's favorite sports figures, and a "Fishers of Men" tie tack. Chris appreciated every gift. He knew that each came from the heart of a man who loved him.

I found it fitting that the gifts ranged from a new basketball to Oswald Chamber's classic book *My Utmost for His Highest.* A beautiful balance between the natural and the spiritual.

This part of the celebration went way beyond my greatest expectations. Yet there was still more to come, something I had not anticipated, a gift as moving and profound as any that had already been offered. Joseph, one of the men there, asked if he could sing a song. I agreed and was surprised to learn that he had written the song just for Christopher only a week before. It was one of the most beautiful ballads about a father and son that I have ever heard. Let me excerpt a piece of the first verse and refrain for you here:

Deep in the stillness
    when the family would sleep,
the Father would call him,
    the Father would speak.

O my beloved, O my sweet,
    tender young boy who the angels keep.
How I love to hold you here in the dark,
    holding the love of a boy in my heart.

The complete song describes the intimate relationship between God the Father and Christ the Son. The lyrics tell of how God can have that same kind of relationship with Christopher—with each of us—because of Christ's love and sacrifice. And we in turn can build our relationships with our sons on the self-sacrificing love of God. The words further urged Christopher and all of us to "listen to the Father, know your Father's plan," because that is where we find true life and maturity.

As the last sounds of Joseph's guitar faded, each man was momentarily lost in his own thoughts. Images of our own fathers and sons flooded our minds. Memories of our past. Visions of our future. All made possible by the Son who died for us all on a hill centuries ago. We were filled with gratitude. Slowly we began to look around at each other. A smile seemed to grace the face of each man in the room. Christopher and the other young men sat in the sweet stillness. They each had that Christmas-morning-and-lots-of-presents-under-the-tree look. Yet they knew that on this night they were receiving presents that would never break or wear out. They knew that these gifts of knowledge and wisdom would be lost only if they chose to let them go.

And I knew it was now time to seal all that had happened. It was time to pray a blessing over Christopher.

CHAPTER 7

BLESSINGS ABUNDANT

James Glenn rose from his seat and walked to the front of the room. He placed a chair in the center of the room and invited Christopher to come and sit in it. James then spoke of the importance of blessing a young man as he grows into manhood. He said that, like light that dispels the darkness, the blessing of a father or mentor can safeguard a young man against much of the world's destructive influence.

James then reminded us about the war between cursing and blessing that rages for every young man's soul. He shared that our heavenly Father's blessing was greater than any worldly curse. He explained:

> In secret, a curse whispers in the young boy's ears, "You will never amount to anything." In response, the Father's blessing loudly proclaims, "Your God has plans for you. Plans of hope and a future."
>
> In secret, a curse whispers in the young boy's ears, "You are rejected and will always be alone." In response, the Father's blessing loudly proclaims, "I will never leave you nor forsake you, and I will provide for you a friend that sticks closer than a brother."

In secret, a curse whispers in the young boy's ears, "You are weak and a failure. You will never succeed in this life." In response, the Father's blessing loudly proclaims, "You can do *all* things through Christ who gives you strength."

Bring Back the Blessing!

When I glanced at Christopher, I thought of all the potential pitfalls that awaited him. All the traps I had blindly fallen into. My heart ached to think of the troubles he would suffer if he chose unwisely. It was almost overwhelming, and I was again struck with the awesome responsibility of fatherhood.

Then I remembered a special time of prayer for my son that occurred over a decade earlier in a unique place and in a unique way. When Christopher was just a baby, I was involved with a statewide prison ministry in Michigan. I would go with a team of men into maximum-security prisons and stay there for four days at a time. Typically, we would sleep inside the prison, walk in the prison yard, and eat in the prison cafeterias. It was not a glamorous ministry, but it provided some of the most meaningful spiritual experiences of my life. The ministry consisted of music, fellowship, small group discussion, personal testimonies, and a series of teachings on the spiritual dimension of life.

Our ministry always had a makeshift chapel in the prison. It was nothing fancy, but we knew that God would honor our efforts to do his will, regardless of where we were. Our speakers would always go into the chapel for prayer before their presentations and return there immediately afterward to thank God for using their words to heal hurting inmates. There were always several men praying in the chapel during the entire four-day ministry, so the presenters had plenty of prayer support.

On one occasion, I was asked to share my personal testimony of what my life had been like without Christ and how it changed once I had committed my life to him. It was painful to honestly recount my mistakes and to share about the many times that sin had been stronger than my desire to do right. I knew, though, that I needed to be vulnerable before these men confined by walls and razor wire. They needed to see that Jesus Christ truly changes lives.

I told the inmates of my life's troubled times and spoke of being near death on several occasions. As I shared about my failures and past sins, I could feel a weight of guilt lifting from my shoulders. The healing continued as I shared about the goodness of God, how he had given me a wonderful wife and, at that time, one fine son. I told of how God had placed me in my own business and had made it possible for my family to have a home of our own.

As I finished my presentation and returned to the chapel, an incredible sense of peace filled my heart. I was thrilled to think that I had really made it out of the snares of my youth.

Suddenly, as I was about to enter the chapel, my joy turned to terror. I was gripped with fear. In my mind, I heard the words, "You might have made it, but your son won't." I stumbled into the chapel and sat down. My mind raced. *My son. My precious Christopher. What will happen to him? What lies in store for him? Car wrecks? Gun shots? The cruel blade of a knife? Will he reject the God who had become so real to me?* I could hardly bear these thoughts.

So I did the only thing that made sense to me. I pitched myself forward on the floor and began to weep. The cold concrete pressed into my face as I called on God's mercy for my son. From the depths of my soul, I cried to God. I begged him to forgive me for all my sins. I begged him to erase any divine judgments that were recorded against me. I begged him to start something new in my family and with my generation. I begged him to touch my son and the children who would come after him, so the evil one could not harm them. My faithful brothers came around me to pray. Their gentle hands on my back brought comfort as I kept crying bitter tears to my Lord. Slowly my fear and grief began to subside.

Then my mind filled with another thought, quieter than the first, but infinitely more powerful: "I will watch over your son." I recognized that voice as the voice of my heavenly Father. With those few words, the peace of God descended on me and turned my grief into rejoicing. I have carried that assurance with me since that amazing day.

"I will watch over your son." These soothing words came back to me as I watched James approach Christopher on his special night.

"I want several of you men to come forward and pray for Christopher," James calmly directed. "But, before we pray, I have a question for you, Chris." Turning to Christopher he asked, "What do you want us to agree with you about when we pray?"

Christopher thought for a moment and then responded, "I want to do what God wants me to do, and I hope he will give me some friends I can walk with along the way."

The rest of us in the room were astounded at his request. Several men moved near my son and began to pray. At first I could only watch. Here were men, firm in their faith, blessing my son. They were pastors, computer experts, heavy equipment operators, and businessmen. All speaking blessings over this young man, my son.

After a few minutes, I took my place in front of Christopher, placed my hands on his head, and prayed. I affirmed him as a man of God. I blessed him in the name of the Lord. As his father, I proclaimed he was my beloved son in whom I was well pleased. I made a public commitment to be there for him whenever he needed me.

Faces glowed. Tears flowed. Hearts were knit together in marvelous ways. Christopher knew that God had already answered part of his prayer. The men who surrounded him were his friends. After the prayer ended, my son rose to his feet and the men in the room hugged him. As we began drifting back to our seats, James spoke again. "We are not quite done here," he said, pointing to the empty chair. "I think the Lord has one more thing in mind."

THE BLESSING OVERFLOWS!

"We came together tonight to bless Christopher," James said with a smile. "But it's obvious that God wants to do more than that. I was raised in a home in the inner city of Detroit, a home without a dad. I'm not complaining, but tonight I realize what I've missed. Can any of you relate?"

Heads nodded all over the room. Our friend had summed up what many were silently feeling.

"Is there anyone here who would like to come up and receive prayer?"

At first no one moved. But then one man slowly walked to the front. He sat in the chair and motioned for the others to pray for him. He sat stiff as a board, tensed against the healing touch of the Lord. His eyes were shut tight. As a boy, he had been abused and later abandoned by his father. A lifetime of confusion, hatred, and bitterness welled up inside him. Some of the men around him seemed to know just how to pray.

"Father, I ask that you would show your love to your son."

"Lord, bless this man whom you died for. Heal his hurts."

Other men spoke affirming words over his life.

"We love you. We appreciate the blessing that you are to us."

"You are a great friend. I am glad that God brought you into my life." With such heartfelt words, ordinary men carried out God's work in this man's life. Restoration. Reconciliation. Healing.

After several minutes, our friend started to relax. A smile came over his face as he squinted at the men huddled around him. Cleansing tears trickled down his cheeks, carrying with them the toxic pain that had been stored inside. Like a river overflowing its banks, the celebration washed over everyone there.

Before we finished, six more men came forward for prayer. Each had a reason for coming. Most felt a deep sense of loss due to their earthly father's inability to love and bless them when they were boys. The last man who asked for prayer had a different need. He said that the celebration revealed his inability to properly love and bless his *own* young son. Through all of the letters, gifts, and skits, he was convinced of his need to show the heavenly Father's love to his son before it was too late. He was not disappointed that night. God did a deep, lasting work in his heart.

To close out our evening, I asked Joseph if he would sing his new song, "O, My Beloved." one last time. After he had sung the beautiful melody, it was time to leave. Amazingly, it was nearly eleven-thirty.

Christopher and I said good-bye to our friends, carefully packed away the memories, and walked out into the star-studded evening. We were tired and drained. Completely empty and completely full at the same time. As we drove away, Chris put his head against the car's headrest and closed his eyes.

"What did you think about tonight, Son?" I asked.

"It was awesome, Dad," Christopher said sleepily. "I can't believe all those men came. You and Mom are something else. I never dreamed I would have a celebration like that."

Then he fell asleep.

I took the long way home that night. I wanted to savor the evening as long as possible, not wanting it to end. My thoughts went to my other precious children: Steven, Jenifer, and Daniel. Their special nights would soon arrive as well.

Then I thought of their future with their children and grandchildren. As I pulled into my driveway, I smiled at the beauty of God's plan of blessing. As long as there are sons and daughters, there must be celebrations. It doesn't have to end.

I gently woke my son and helped him upstairs to bed.

"Good night, Son," I whispered. "I sure do love you."

"Thanks Dad, I love you too," he said with a yawn. "Man, that celebration was awesome."

Keep Growing Him, Lord!

The day following the celebration was a typical summer day at our home. At about seven-thirty, my youngest son, Daniel Elijah, made sure I knew it was morning. Prying open my eyelids, he whispered, "Come on, Dad, get up! Dad, let's play!" Soon the rest of the family shifted into high gear. The lawn mower roared, basketballs bounced, children argued and played.

Christopher was the last one to get up that day. The excitement and lack of sleep the night before had taken their toll. When he finally came downstairs, his brothers and sister surrounded him with questions about what had happened the night before. It was great to see Christopher hug his mother and excitedly share with her and his siblings about his celebration.

Kathleen began reading the letters the men had written. She made it only halfway through the first letter before her tears began to flow. Steven, Jenifer and Daniel listened intently to stories of exploding soda bottles, bags of shelled corn, and a special song. They knew that they, too, would have a celebration one day.

Christopher carefully made a list of each man who attended, jotted what they had shared with him, and planned to send each one a personal thank-you note.

Watching the wonderful mayhem, I was filled with awe and thanksgiving. I paid special attention to Christopher and wondered, *How will the celebration touch his life? Was it really a turning point or just a nice party?*

It has been over three years since Christopher's celebration, so I've had ample time to observe his behavior. There have been some interesting developments…

For the first few days after the celebration, Christopher seemed to be his usual self. But as several weeks went by, I began seeing a definite change in some key areas of his life. His approach to household chores, for instance. He had always tried to be obedient when it came to work around the house, but he had a hard time remembering to do his assignments without being asked. Also, when he was younger, he'd typically do a half-hearted job whenever he had work to do. Those were the days when, if we asked him to clean his room, he'd reluctantly agree—and then simply stuff his closet full of everything from tennis shoes to damp towels. Fortunately, this is one of the areas that changed following the celebration. His work ethic improved. Chris started completing his chores without being asked. Not only did he do them, but also he did them with more attention to detail than before.

Chris also seemed more eager to take on new challenges. For example, a few days after the celebration, I discovered that a tire on my truck had gone flat. Typically, my children would stand by and watch me work on this type of project, but not that morning. Christopher volunteered to change the tire. I confess I had my doubts about his ability to handle the task. The spare was located under the car, and the jack was one of the new ones that baffles even the best mechanics. Nonetheless, my son was adamant about changing the tire, so I agreed to let him do it. This time, I was the one who watched. I gave him some brief counsel about safety before letting him begin and, to my pleasant surprise, he read the instructions in the car owner's manual, following the proper procedures from start to finish. He was rightfully proud when the job was completed. So was I.

During the past three years, I have seen a continued improvement in his ability to work effectively, despite the fact that he has more school and other activities that compete for his attention. Now that he has a car, Chris has accepted the responsibility to regularly drive into the city to take care of Grandpa Hayes's lawn in the summer and shovel snow in the winter. Clearly, he learned from the celebration to accept work as an important responsibility of a man.

Another area that changed over the years is his relationship with his younger brothers and sister. In the past, Chris seemed to tolerate them but certainly didn't treat them as well as he treated his friends. Since the celebration, though, he has gotten progressively more attentive and friendly toward each of them. It is especially gratifying to see him interact with his younger sister, Jenifer. She is sometimes left out of the fun when the boys get rough with each other. At times, Jeni has rightfully lamented that she had no one to play with. Christopher's kindness to her has brought about a change in her attitude. She is happier now that she knows he cares for her.

Still another area of change that Kathy and I noticed has been in Chris's approach to worship and other aspects of his relationship with God. In our Sunday church services, we often begin with a time of praise and worship. More often than not, the adults in the service sing and praise the Lord while many of the young people passively sit in their seats. We have been thrilled to see Christopher join in the worship and really enjoy it.

One of the most satisfying aspects of the new Christopher comes in the area of identity and self-confidence. He has always been great to have for a son. However, sometimes he was too timid and compliant for his own good. Kathy and I now notice that he shares his views more easily on a variety of issues. He speaks with a new boldness and assurance, believing he has something of value to share. In his earlier years, Chris was rather shy in school and unsure of his own abilities. In the past few years he has grown into a fine athlete and confidently plays basketball for a class-A high school. He makes friends easier now and yet still holds onto very high standards of conduct. At a time when many of his peers are experimenting with sex, drugs, and alcohol, Chris has remained committed to making good choices. Predictably, this has brought some persecution from others at school. Just as predictably, others are drawn to Chris to learn why he has the courage to resist.

Along with Christopher's newfound confidence has come an increased ability to laugh and enjoy life. It's important for parents and young men alike to understand that maturity doesn't mean "no fun." Too many adults seem to lose their sense of humor as they grow older. God intends for joy to accompany us on our journey to mature manhood. Joy and laughter are not childish; rather they are wonderful signs that a man's faith, hope, and life are all pointing in the proper direction. In the years since his celebration, Christopher laughs more often and more deeply than before.

I want to be very clear about these changes. Christopher has not mastered the art of manhood at the ripe old age of sixteen! Like the rest of us, he still occasionally does a poor job with a work project, is less than kind to his siblings, and has doubts about his future. The big difference now is that he recognizes these problems as matters of maturity rather than manhood. In other words, he knows that, as a man, he should continue to strive for excellence in these areas. When his performance is not what it should be, he doesn't mentally slide all the way back into boyhood again, nor does he question his manhood. Instead, he simply accepts that he has to improve in some specific areas of his life. This allows him to prayerfully pursue the achievable goal of maturity, rather than struggle to attain something that he already has—his manhood.

Please understand that not all of Christopher's positive qualities are a result of the celebration. His mother and I have done our best to teach him right from wrong for many years. To the best of our ability, we provided Christopher with instruction about family relationships, work, worship, and many other aspects of maturity since he was very little. I am sure that some of the lessons are just now beginning to sink in. Celebrations will not instantly create a perfect man. They are not designed to. However, I am convinced that something wonderful happened deep inside this young man during the ceremony. Was it an imparting of godly gifts when the older men prayed for Christopher, or did the celebration release qualities he always had within him? Was it the letters or gifts or skits that changed my son's approach to life? Or was it a combination of all these things? While only God knows the exact answer, it is obvious that something significant changed in my son following the celebration. The Lord did a deep work, and by his grace, Christopher has grown and matured. He has become a better man. A celebration will do the same for the young men in your life as well.

Christopher is not the only person who changed. The celebration changed me, too. It has caused me to view each of my children differently. I now see them as wonderful works in progress. I now try to take more time with them each day to talk, play, listen, and love. Because of my son's celebration, I have become a better father. The other men who attended the celebration have changed also. Most have held celebrations for their own sons and have refocused their attention on what is of primary importance in life—their God and their families.

CHAPTER 8

BOYHOOD TO MANHOOD: WHY CELEBRATIONS WORK

In the years following Christopher's event, I spent a great deal of time thinking about the celebration concept, its applications, and its impact. Initially, I questioned whether it would work. In other words, would the celebration actually help young males in their transition into mature manhood? After participating in numerous celebrations and seeing their impact on those being celebrated and those in attendance, my questions began to change. My original question of "Will it work?" soon changed to "Why does it work?"

Over time I have come to some conclusions. But first let me tell a couple of quick stories to demonstrate why celebrations are so desperately needed in our society today.

THE PAIN OF NO ANSWER

A friend of mine, Charles, recently shared a profound incident that happened to him when he was growing up. When he was about four-teen, Charles was riding in a car with his father. Since it was just the two of them, my friend thought it was a great time to ask his dad about something that had been troubling him for several months. After traveling a few miles, Charles mustered up sufficient courage to pop the question.

"Dad, when do I become a man?" he asked expectantly.

Charles told me he hoped his dad would respond with something that sounded as if it came out of a Hollywood script. He anticipated that his dad would look lovingly into his young eyes, pat his shoulder with a strong right hand, and then explain exactly how a boy becomes a man. Sadly, that did not happen. Instead, Charles's father did something that amazed him. His dad chuckled, and without so much as a sideways glance at his son, changed the subject.

That was it.

Charles explained to me that even though the incident took only moments to tell, it took years to overcome. He sadly told me of the painful struggles with his own identity as a man and how the uncertainties had guided his choices in life. He went on to share that he had wasted much of his life experimenting with sex, drugs, and violent sports, looking for something to signify that he had arrived at "manhood."

My friend's story didn't surprise me. In fact, it confirmed the desperate need young men have for a solid answer to the "manhood question." Charles's scenario is all too common in today's society. It is replayed over and over again. Predictably, a boy in his early teens asks a logical question about his impending manhood, and the man in his life—if one exists—doesn't have a clear-cut response. This pattern doesn't have to continue, but men need to have a serious change of heart if we are going to turn the pattern around.

The Confusion of Changing "Mile-Markers"

Recently, I was sharing the celebration concept with another man and was amazed at his response. He adamantly told me, "Everyone knows there's no way a thirteen-year-old boy is a man!" This gentleman then offered several rambling explanations about the legal drinking age, the age for military service, the age for young people to legally drive, and so on. I found it fascinating that each of these ages of "accountability" or "adulthood" was different. There was not consistency in any of them. Not only did the "age of accountability" differ from state to state, but it also had been changed many times in recent years. This man's words simply underscored the confusion our society has concerning entry into adulthood. Gordon Dalbey writes about this sad perplexity:

> What does my own culture offer as a validation of manhood? The driver's license at sixteen; the freedom at eighteen to join the army, attend pornographic movies, and to buy cigarettes and beer. The message is clear: becoming a man means operating a powerful machine, killing other men, masturbating, destroying your lungs, and getting drunk.
>
> We are lost males, all of us: cast adrift from the community of men, cut off from our masculine heritage—abandoned to machines, organizations, fantasies, and drugs.[1]

---

1. Gordon Dalbey, *Healing the Masculine Soul* (Dallas: Word, 1988), quoted in Gary Wilde, *Mentoring: An Example to Follow* (Colorado Springs: ChariotVictor, 1997), 13-4.

I tried to tell the man that when I was in my teens, the drinking age in Michigan was changed from twenty-one to eighteen. This may have been due in part to the fact that we were drafting eighteen-year-old men—or were they boys?—and sending them to kill and die in Southeast Asia, but they couldn't legally drink a beer when at home on leave. Also, during that time period, a sixteen-year-old could drive a car twenty-four hours a day. He simply got his license and that was it. Today, both of these ages have changed again. The legal drinking age is now back to twenty-one and, while a sixteen-year-old can still get his license, he can't legally drive after midnight. None of this seemed to matter to him.

When this man finished his half-baked lecture, I asked him one simple question: "Then exactly when *does* a boy become a man?" Like my friend Charles's father, he had no answer. He finally sputtered that he really didn't know, but he was sure that it wasn't at age thirteen.

The Powerful Solution: It's a Declaration!

In reality, the solution to Charles's and every other young male's problem is simple yet profound: A young male becomes a man *when the elders of his society declare him to be one.*

This was true for Sidimo, just as it was true for White Fox, Marcus, and David. In those cultures, young males accepted their parents' and other elders' declarations about manhood as truth. They then began to live according to these new adult expectations.

Now I readily admit that it's wise to withhold certain privileges and responsibilities from young men. I am not advocating that we lower the legal age for certain activities such as drinking, voting, serving in the military, or getting married. Many young people are not ready to handle such things without counsel, mentoring, and support from others. This is not because they aren't men; rather it is because they are not mature. However, if we, as a society, continue to consciously or unconsciously connect manhood with any of these events, then we unintentionally encourage our young males to think—and act—like children during their early teen years. We condition our young people to believe that legal drinking, driving, or having sex are somehow rites of passage into adulthood by themselves. In this frame of mind, is it any wonder that our young people act like kids far into their teens and twenties? Also, is it any wonder that our young men are so drawn to these activities? Could it be that they are trying to attain their manhood earlier than when their society tells them they can have it?

It makes infinitely more sense for us to condition our young males to accept their manhood at an early age and then help them grow into maturity. Then they will be ready to make good choices about such matters when they arrive at whatever age the privileges are granted.

We must realize that young males like my friend Charles, and Jason at the beginning of this book, are literally dying to hear an adult simply and confidently answer their questions about manhood, set the course, and then cheer as they run the race toward maturity. A celebration is the one event that will mark that special day of transition from boyhood into manhood. It is the day that will answer all the questions about "when." From that day on, the questions of our young males will focus on how to act as a men, rather than on when or if they will become one.

The Cornerstone of Manhood

I am convinced that a celebration leads to mature manhood just as, in orthodox Christian teaching, salvation leads to sanctification. A person becomes a Christian at the moment he or she accepts Christ by faith and is thereby born anew spiritually. This person's rightful position and identity is as a spiritual child in God's family. The person can never be more of a Christian than he is at the moment of acceptance. He will become much more *mature,* but not more of a Christian. Scripture does not teach that we earn our Christianity by degrees, levels, or ages. It teaches that acceptance of Christ is the door through which one enters into the faith and is fully accepted into the fold.

Naturally, the new convert must be taught what the works of a mature Christian are and how to do them. These works include a renewal of the mind and heart, which leads to changes in one's attitudes, behaviors, communication, and worldview. Sanctification is a growth process that aims at spiritual maturity. Its goal is to grow spiritual babes into spiritual adults who are mature in every area of life. Clearly each person goes through a process of maturity; however, the process cannot begin until one has become a child of God. Before any maturing takes place, new converts must accept that a miraculous transformation occurred and they have transitioned from one condition into another totally different one.

In a like manner, a young male must first accept his *calling* into manhood if he is ever to do the *works* of a mature man. Obviously, a teenage boy is not fully developed physically, mentally, emotionally, or spiritually. However, at his celebration, he is formally and publicly welcomed into manhood. From loving elders, he learns that he was created to be a man and that there are good works prepared in advance for him to do (see Ephesians 2:8-10). Once the elders open the door to manhood, the boy experiences a miraculous change in that his goal is now to grow into maturity as a man. The celebration acts as the door into manhood, just as salvation is the door to sanctification. After a boy walks through the door to manhood, the rest of the journey to clearer identity and maturity begins in earnest.

If, on the other hand, he never walks through the door to manhood, he is condemned to wander for years outside of his intended domain. The teen is then left to stumble into his future by default rather than boldly pursuing it by design with the help of mature men. Without a transitional event to mark a boy's passage into manhood, he is sentenced to spend many years trying to discover ways to affirm and confirm his coming of age. Sadly, he will look for an *action* rather than for an *event* to mark his transition. Our young people today are vainly substituting their first cigarette, drink, sexual encounter, theft, gang fight, or even murder for a true transitional celebration event. How much better it is for mature adults to lead our young males into a defining rite of passage—a celebration that makes it clear that they have entered the realm and the ranks of manhood.

Celebrations Answer a Boy's Profound Questions About Identity

Here's the second reason that a celebration has such a positive impact on men: A celebration answers critical questions about our male identities. Contemporary man struggles so much with his personal identity and purpose. This creates dissatisfaction with life that affects our wives, children, and everyone around us.

I am convinced that the common midlife crisis that seems to afflict so many men in our society has its roots in a lack of identity and painful uncertainties about our manhood. As a man in my late forties, I can attest to the changes that influence a man's physiological and emotional being. Clearly, we are not the same as we were in our teens, twenties, or thirties. At this age, we realize that much of our life is behind us and the part that remains is moving rapidly forward. This is cause for some heartfelt questions and reflections. *Where am I going? What have I really accomplished? What lies ahead?* These are very real issues that challenge all men in their autumn years. However, much of the turmoil that men experience in their midlives is more related to their pasts than to their futures.

As a result, the cause of the stereotypical midlife crisis is often misdiagnosed. For generations we have said that the man in his forties or fifties who leaves his wife for a twenty-year-old woman and new sports car is trying to regain his lost youth. Or another way to describe this type of illogical behavior is to say that he is reverting from manhood into his "second" childhood.

I don't think that's what is really going on. You see, this man *never made the transition out of childhood and into manhood.* The hectic years of getting an education, entering into marriage, raising children, making money, and so on, have distracted him from addressing this basic life issue. However, he now awakens to the realization that despite his many accomplishments, activities, possessions, and responsibilities, he is still not whole. He intuitively knows that something vital is missing from his life, so he sets out to find it, not as an adult, but as a boy still searching for that elusive measure of manhood.

If he fails to correctly identify what is missing, he will inevitably pursue "it" in all the wrong places. At the very time when the man's wisdom, experience, and other aspects of life are at their peak, he falls into a series of predictable traps that could ruin his life's legacy. We all know men and their families who have suffered through these tumultuous times. Celebrations will prevent this from happening to our sons as they enter midlife.

Obviously, many middle-aged men won't pursue new love relationships or fancy cars, and so outwardly they seem very solid. However, many still wrestle with their identities as men. Many, like my friend Charles, cannot answer the question, "Have I arrived as a man?" For this reason, even seventy-year-old fathers can help their middle-aged sons with a celebration that answers that universal question with a healing "Yes! You have arrived."

It's Never Too Late

I'd like to conclude this chapter by relating some things that may help you with your reaction to this rite-of-passage concept. I hope you are very excited about the celebration idea. I have never spoken to anyone who wasn't overwhelmingly positive toward it. However, upon reflection, you may also feel some sadness—perhaps even some anger—that no one held this type of event for you when you were younger. You may be imagining how your life would have been different if your parents had helped you transition into adulthood with a celebratory blessing.

Or maybe your parents abandoned or abused you, leaving you to move into the adult years with deep scars rather than with affirmations of love for you and confirmations of your growing maturity. At the other end of the spectrum, it may be that your children have grown and moved away from home, and you're feeling regret that you missed opportunities to celebrate them when they were younger.

I have good news for you! It is never too late to be healed, and it is never too late to be a blessing to your own children, regardless of how old they are.

To you who are still hurt by the lack of care you received from your natural parents, please know that God has promised to be a father to the fatherless (Psalm 68:5). He is capable of healing your wounds and turning your sorrows into joy (Psalm 30:11). You can call on him to meet your every need, even those from many years ago. If this describes you, then I suggest that you begin to share how you feel with your wife, a good friend, pastor, priest, or counselor. As we found at Christopher's celebration, many men are bound with anger, bitterness, and a sense of sorrow over what did or did not happen to them in the past. Just talking about it helps. Talking and then praying about it will definitely open new doors of healing for you.

Also, if you regret never having helped your older children transition into adulthood, know it is *not* too late. Your words can still bless your children, no matter how old they are. Your sons and daughters still need to hear you say "I love you" and feel your concern for them.

If you have older children or even grown children, how do you bless them? It's simple. Pick up the phone, jump in your car, or get on a plane. Do whatever it takes to reconnect with your precious offspring. You may feel a bit rusty, but the blessing you'll bring them will still have an incredibly powerful impact upon their lives—and upon yours as well.

Regardless of their ages, plan the celebration that you didn't have when they were younger. You will be amazed at how God will bless you, your children, and your children's children through just one special night of celebration.

CHAPTER 9

FOUNDATIONS FOR YOUR OWN CELEBRATION

When the celebration for my son ended, the most common response I heard from the men who attended was, "I can't wait to do this for my son!" The hearts of all who attended burned with passion about the importance of this type of ceremony. As they spoke with others, that wonderful fire spread rapidly. Men's groups from around the world have contacted me, asking for information on how to hold celebrations for the boys in their lives.

Numerous youth pastors have asked how they can implement this concept for the boys in their churches, especially those who are without fathers at home. Single mothers have asked how they can host a celebration for their sons, especially if they lack the support of the boy's father. As a result of these inquiries, I have had the honor of planning and attending many celebrations over the past few years. From these experiences, I am convinced that the ingredients I list on the following pages are foundational issues that must be considered when planning a celebration.

Knowing the Celebration Essentials

I believe a properly planned celebration is an essential part of every young man's life. This means that a celebration is not merely an option; it is a necessity. There just isn't an alternative to acknowledging a boy's transition into manhood. A big birthday party won't do it. A trip to Disney World won't do it. Parents, grandparents, or other concerned elders must accept responsibility for planning and hosting a celebration for each young male in their lives.

The four questions below are the typical ones I'm asked when people first start thinking about planning a celebration. I hope my answers will give you some practical guidance as you move ahead with your own celebration plans.

What Is the Best Age?

There is something special about affirming manhood during the early teen years. Many cultures throughout history have identified the preteen and teen years as the time when their boys make the transition into manhood. In our modern culture, we clearly recognize that the teen years are a special period but, unfortunately, we have not known what to do with them! Rather than fearing this period as a time of impending rebellion, we can now begin to celebrate it as a time of transition.

As I mentioned in the previous chapter, when we seize the opportunity to help our youth move into adulthood, we prevent them from having to create their own rites of passage—rites usually marked with conflict and experimentation with so-called grown-up things, such as drugs, alcohol, and sex. When we help them establish their God-ordained internal identities, we help them avoid creating false identities through externals such as wild hairstyles, body piercing, tattoos, and counterculture clothing. When we communicate that there is a proper time and method for them to "grow up" and become self-supporting, we help our young people avoid poorly planned schemes for independence, such as dropping out of school or running away from home.

We parents will close the door on many of our teens' potential problems—struggles with low self-esteem, poor self-image, lack of purpose, despair, cynicism, and rebellion—by our attention to their rites of passage into adulthood. Since these problems often arise during the early teen years, I am convinced that our modern-day Sidimos, Davids, and Jasons will benefit from celebrations that occur between the ages of thirteen and sixteen.

But what about those parents who have sons that are older? Have these youth missed out on the opportunity to grow into mature adulthood? Not at all! This type of celebration will be extremely effective for a young man of eighteen, twenty-one, or even older. Indeed, this ceremony can be a life-changing event for men who have even reached their thirties, forties, and beyond. The old saying "better late than never" definitely applies here. The real key, though, is that mature men be involved in the celebration to confirm, affirm, and bless the celebrant's manhood.

While this type of ceremony can be connected to a teen's birthday, it may also be linked with other special events occurring later in a young man's life, such as graduating from high school, voting for the first time, entering college, graduating from college, landing a first job, having a truly meaningful bachelor party, or experiencing the birth of his first child. In other words, you don't have to wait until a particular birthday rolls around to host the celebration. Use any opportunity you have, as soon as you can. You and your son will be glad you did. Our entire society will benefit as well.

What Is Mom's Role?

Another central issue concerns the role of a boy's mother in his celebration. Kathleen and I agree that whenever possible, a mom should help plan the ceremony and spend some special time with her son prior to the gathering. She may do such things as take him to lunch or prepare his favorite meal before the evening's celebration. Also, she may want to write him a keepsake letter that he can open when he returns home. However, we have concluded that *it is better if the mother not host or attend her son's celebration.*

I realize this is a very emotional subject that takes some time to think through. Some moms initially bristle at the suggestion that they not attend. They reason that they have spent the last thirteen-plus years carrying, nursing, nurturing, comforting, feeding, and generally caring for this youngster and therefore deserve to be part of his special day. I acknowledge that, in many homes, mom has been the most significant woman and perhaps that most significant person in her boy's life. Nothing will ever change that. Nevertheless, a celebration marking a boy's transition to manhood is an event best accomplished in the presence and under the guidance of other men.

Kathleen actually came to this conclusion first. She believes there must be a time when a mother releases her son into the care of the men in her home, extended family, church, or broader community. From her perspective, releasing does not mean abandoning or ignoring the boy, nor does it mean that the boy will no longer need his mother. It simply means that there is a change in the mother-son relationship. I turned Kathleen's thoughts on this subject into the following note to a son. It might help both women and men understand the concept of "releasing" from a mother's perspective:

My son,

Since before you were born, I have nurtured you, cared for you, and protected you. But now it is time for you to take an important step. Today I am releasing you to become the man you were created to become. It is time for you to take more responsibility for your own actions. I will always love you as my son, but from this day forward, I will also respect you as a man. I will no longer try to control your actions, but I will work with you to think through your future. You have a special place in my heart. Now go for this short time to discover your special place among the men. When your celebration is over, come back and share with me what you have learned and who you have become.

Your Mother

I greatly appreciate Kathleen's perspective on this issue. She really helped me sort through the emotions involved so we could arrive at the best conclusion for celebrations.

Husbands and fathers should be especially sensitive to the mother's feelings before, during, and after her son's celebration. Dads can help moms understand and enjoy all that takes place at her son's celebration by videotaping the proceedings and by taking some photos as well. It's an emotional time for everyone involved, so some extra concern, communication, and caring can help the rite of passage be a smooth and rewarding event for the whole family.

Does It Have to Be a Spiritual Event?

I want to emphasize the fact that a rite of passage like this is a profoundly spiritual event. We must not allow it to become just a fancy birthday party, devoid of spirituality, God, or religious foundations. This is a time for parents to intentionally decide who they are and what they believe. Remember, there is no such thing as an unbeliever. Everyone believes in something or someone as the ultimate authority in his or her life. This ultimate authority is the one counted on in times of trouble and looked to as a provider. This ultimate authority also determines right and wrong, thereby guiding many of life's decisions.

For some people, this ultimate authority is self, and for others it is some form of government. For me, and millions of others, someone else is in charge of this universe. This "someone else" left a clear account of what is right and what is wrong, showing us how to deal with life and death on the earth. The account is found in the Bible, and that someone, God, responds to prayer and any sincere attempt to reach him. He offers life to a world that sees too much death. He ordains that each child is born and has purpose, direction, and value. This is my worldview, a solid belief that will carry me through all of life's joys and sorrows. But these are issues that all mothers and fathers must settle in their own thinking before launching their sons into such an uncertain world via a celebratory rite of passage. You cannot give your son what you don't have.

I have heard many well-meaning parents say that they didn't want to push their children toward any particular religion. Instead, they wanted to let their young people "find their own way." In my view, that is the most irresponsible position a parent could take with life's most important issue. Imagine the drastic impact on a child whose parents took this approach to some of the lesser issues of life. A young boy with no instruction on hygiene would never brush his teeth or comb his hair. Too much bother. A young boy with no guidelines on diet would certainly live—and prematurely die—on junk food. Tastes better. A young boy left to decide about his own education would probably never enter school. Too much trouble. No parent in his right mind would think of abdicating his responsibility for instruction in these basic matters. How much more should they direct their precious children into a relationship with a loving God?

The point here is simple. Parents must take sufficient time to determine their own position on spirituality before they attempt to host a celebration for their sons. Once their own spiritual foundation is laid, the parents can begin to share it with their children as part of their upbringing. A powerful culmination of this sharing can take place during the celebration when a son is released to pursue God for himself, as a man. The living and active faith seen in his parents will make the celebration and time of prayer at the end infinitely more powerful than if there is no faith seen at home. As a final thought here, please understand that parents don't have to be spiritual superstars for this to be genuine. They simply need to have a real desire to know God and follow him to the best of their abilities. This sincerity will be seen and admired by their son.

How Will Prayer Play a Part?

If there were ever a time to set aside distractions and spend time in reflective prayer for your family, it is during the time prior to the celebration. There is no substitute! The impact of prayer will be evident in many ways during the celebration. Parents should prayerfully consider who to invite, where to have the gathering, and what to include on the agenda for their son's celebration. These are all-important aspects of the event, and nothing should be taken for granted. This is why the foundation for every aspect of the celebration must be prayer. Prayer will let the men know what to write, say, and give to your young man. Prayer will seal the blessing for your son when the celebration ends. Prayer is the greatest assurance you can have that your celebration will accomplish its eternal goals.

And when it comes to goals, you may be wondering about the best "size" of celebration to aim for. Our society continually preaches that bigger is better than small, fancy is better than plain, and enough money will make anything succeed. Don't get caught up in any of this nonsense when it comes to your son's celebration. A prayerfully focused celebration held in a cement-block basement and attended by just a few men will be infinitely more powerful than some godless grand production held in a fancy conference center. Never forget that these are God's children we are celebrating and preparing for adulthood. Without the spiritual element, any celebration will fall far short of its potential impact. Quality, not quantity, is key here. Keep praying about it!

Now let's get down to the details the celebration itself. What specific plans will you need to make in advance? What particular arrangements and activities will you need to consider?

MANAGING THE EVENT ITSELF

Naturally, there are many options, and you should feel free to be creative. However, I do have some general suggestions that can help assure that the basic elements are well cared for in advance.

Choose a Practical Location

Remember that the celebration is primarily designed to allow our young men to receive blessings, affirmations, and encouragement from older men. Thus the event may be as simple or as elaborate as you choose. The impact will come from the depth of what is shared rather than from the setting itself. Therefore, many different locations can be appropriate, including a home, hotel, church, campsite, or rented meeting hall.

If your boy has a favorite location that would be appropriate for a celebration, then go there. I recall a wonderful letter that I recently received from a missionary in Nigeria. This man had gotten a copy of an early manuscript of this book and wrote to tell me of his plans to celebrate his son's transition into manhood. He was planning to host the event at his son's favorite spot, a river in Nigeria that was complete with waterfalls. He and his son would journey there in a Land Rover, accompanied by a few of their male friends. The agenda for their special day was to spend some time relaxing by the water, cooking his son's favorite meal over the open fire, and then sharing some letters and gifts from other men. Pick a location that will comfortably hold the number of people you invite and allow for sufficient room for all of your planned activities.

Timing

Just as there are many alternatives for where to hold a celebration, there are lots of options for when one can be scheduled. You can plan yours for any day of the week, but you need to consider work, school, air travel for guests, and other potential hindrances. Be sure to allow sufficient time so that you are not rushed. This once-in-a-lifetime event must not be overshadowed by anything else.

Arrange for Refreshments

It's a nice touch when some refreshments are provided during the celebration. They may be eaten before or after the event. Refreshments may include a formal dinner, just snacks, a cake, beverages, or any other combination that is appropriate for your boy's special event. But please don't think that you must have a catered dinner to make the celebration a success. In fact, food and refreshments are add-ons to the celebration. They are not essentials.

Contact the Guests

The number of men attending the celebration may range from three to thirty. I would discourage a gathering larger than that, as it creates problems with space and overextends the length of the event. Here again, more is not necessarily better. Your boy will be blessed that just a few men cared enough to attend his special event. He will also know whether some came simply out of obligation or whether some of the men are sitting there preoccupied with other things.

Invitations should be sent at least two weeks before the event. However, four weeks notice, or more, is preferable in order to allow time for the adjustment of busy schedules. You can use my letter as a model or write your own. Just be sure to include place, time, and all other details. Don't assume that the men will understand the vision initially. Lovingly explain what you are doing, give the reasons why, and state specifically what you need from them.

Plan for Skits and Dramas

Skits and dramas can be powerful tools for teaching life lessons. They take the old adage of "a picture is worth a thousand words" to a new dimension: A *demonstration* is worth a thousand pictures! This means that whatever skits you choose must be designed to lovingly and powerfully teach lessons your unique son will need for the future. So let me head off any potential skit problems with a few dos and don'ts:

- *DO be very creative in your skit design.* There is no shortage of challenges that we face in life, so there are countless life lessons that can be powerfully portrayed in a skit or drama. Today's man must deal with emotions, friendship, work, education, choices, purity, faith, and a wide variety of other family issues. Any and all of these are great foundations for skits. They don't have to be funny or elaborate to be effective. But they can be very, very creative. Just make sure they are appropriate to your son's age, maturity level, and life experiences.

- *DO select your participants wisely.* Make sure that each person involved is credible and able to handle the tasks assigned. By this I mean don't have an avowed atheist attempt to portray a message about the importance of a spiritual foundation for life! This will not be well received. Also, be sure you don't assign someone to be part of a skit if he tends to want to attract attention to himself. Putting a frustrated would-be comedian in front of a dozen other people is a recipe for disaster. The focus must be on the lesson, not on the people taking part in the skit. Select participants who are levelheaded, outgoing, and not prone to act silly. Then make sure they have time to prepare for their part.

- *DON'T substitute skits for personal interaction.* Remember that skits are not a substitute for a man talking, face to face, with his son about important life issues or problems that he may be facing. This should be an ongoing part of your relationship with him. A skit could never take the place of such interaction.

- *DON'T make the skit your ultimate "weapon."* A skit is not the appropriate vehicle for "finally" getting a particular point across to your son. It's not to be used as a weapon to browbeat a young man. A frustrated parent may have been talking with his son for years about the need for better grooming, industriousness, spirituality, or any other subject. The night of his special celebration is not the time to ram the point home one more time. This would be a lecture in disguise. Please don't bother. It would cheapen the rest of the event and probably ensure another few years of noncompliance by your son. I encourage you to trust the celebration process and allow your son to grow toward maturity after it is over.

- *DON'T design a skit that would embarrass your son.* Avoid humiliating your son by pointing out his weaknesses or his past failures. For example, if he has been in trouble with authority in school, a skit about respecting your teachers would be a bad idea. Also, if he has struggled with or gotten caught with drugs or alcohol, then a skit about the dangers of substance abuse would be inappropriate. The young man would perceive this as an attempt to embarrass him in front of respected elders. Clearly, that's not your goal.

- *DON'T gloss over the details.* Good skits take detailed planning. As the host, your role in the skit process is threefold. First, prayerfully design skits that will teach and minister to your son at his celebration. Second, prayerfully select the right people to be in the skit. Third, carefully write out the skit, along with the primary lessons to be covered, detailing what props are needed, so that your participants clearly understand your vision and their responsibilities. And here is a final hint: When you design your skits, be sure that *all the props will be available when you need them.* You don't want to be making changes at the last second because a prop is unavailable, broken, or just overlooked.

Be Open to Including Alternative Activities

For various reasons, some people will not feel comfortable with skits and dramas at their son's celebration. Either they are unsure of their abilities to perform in the skits, or they determine that their son will not respond favorably to a skit. In these instances, there are many alternatives that can make the celebration interesting, powerful, and memorable for your son.

One alternative is to prepare a poster board or sheet of paper with your son's name at the top. Pass the board around to the attendees and have them write two words that describe your son. Words like *diligent, strong, brave, smart,* and *loving* will greatly encourage your son and help him see himself as others see him.

Another alternative is for the dad or grandfather to share positive stories and remembrances about the son from his childhood. These must be positive and not embarrassing for the young man. His first fish, first building project, or a particular act of kindness or bravery would all remind your son that he has had a positive impact on his family and his world since he first arrived.

Yet another alternative or addition to skits and dramas is to present your son with a scrapbook of his photos and accomplishments from the past. This type of presentation would make an excellent foundation for the young man's future.

The bottom line is this: The celebration should be designed in a way that creates powerful, positive memories for your son. He will remember the sights, sounds, messages, people, and emotions for a lifetime. Take time to design the celebration with this in mind.

As a final foundational thought, remember that the underlying motive for the celebration is love. Thankfully, love covers a multitude of sins, errors, and mistakes, so you don't need to worry if something doesn't go quite as planned. Love will take care of it. As you plan your celebration please just relax and follow your heart. It is going to be great!

CHAPTER 10

CELEBRATION FOR A SECOND SON

Steven, my second son, was born three years after Christopher entered this world. He came very close to not being born at all. When Kathleen was pregnant with him, she began to have some serious complications, including hard contractions at just over twelve weeks. As a result, her physician put her on strict bed rest for the remaining six months of the pregnancy. Being up on her feet for even a little while would put our unborn son's life in the gravest peril.

This was the most difficult time of our young married life. I had recently started my own human resource development company and had to travel extensively or risk losing our only client. This left Kathy to watch over three-year-old Christopher as she lay flat on her back for the entire day. Friends and family came over each day to assist with chores, cook meals, pray, and entertain Christopher. The process challenged both our faith and our endurance. We learned to pray without ceasing, as numerous times we had to rush Kathy to the hospital to stop the contractions. One particular night we had two frightful trips to the emergency room as new complications jeopardized the lives of both mother and baby.

I gained an incredible amount of respect for my lovely wife during this time. I cannot imagine spending six days in bed with little to occupy my time—let alone six months! However, my wife possesses a powerful combination of mother's love and warrior's heart. For her the pregnancy was not convenient nor was it enjoyable. Instead, it was painful, restricting, and frustrating. If she wanted to end the pain, she could simply get out of bed and go for a walk. The baby would have been lost, but she could have gotten on with her life. That is not how God created her. She sacrificed six months of her life to secure the life of our son, Steven David Molitor.

We warmly recall that during her time of bed rest, Kathy's physician wanted us to keep track of the baby's movements within the womb. This was the primary means of determining the impact of all the complications on his health. Using this method, "healthy" meant that Steven would give mom a kick at least ten times during the course of a day. Kathy usually recorded ten kicks within the first hour of the day. Steven, within the womb, let us know that he was alive and well. He entered the world some six months later and has not stopped kicking up his heels since.

THE ANTICIPATION BUILDS

Steven was just over ten years old when we held Christopher's celebration. He was fascinated by the stories of the skits as well as the gifts Christopher received. I was quick to tell him that his special day would arrive in due time. During the following three years, Steven went through many of the typical changes for a boy his age. He is taller and stronger. His voice now sounds like a baritone rather than a tenor. Girls have caught his eye. He thinks about the future now instead of just the present.

It was fascinating to watch as Steven's view of his upcoming celebration changed as well. Soon after his older brother's special day, Steven would ask me when his day would arrive. At that point, the underlying motivation was more focused on a gathering and gifts than on maturity and manhood. This was certainly in line with the thinking of a ten-year-old boy. However, in the months preceding his celebration, Steven began to grasp the true meaning of the celebration concept. He no longer talked about what he would *get,* in terms of things; instead he began to consider who he was to *become* as a person.

Steven was not the only one who had three years to think about his celebration. As his father, I spent a great deal of time pondering and praying about his special day. I wanted it to be unique and created just for Steven. After having such a powerful celebration for Christopher, I prayed that Steven's event would somehow hold the same wonder for us all.

That prayer was answered.

THE SPECIAL DAY ARRIVES

What an incredible joy it was for me when Steven's celebration day finally arrived. His day was unique and yet built upon some traditions begun three years earlier when Christopher was the guest of honor. On his special day, Steven and I had a fine dinner with Grandpa Hayes and then made our way to the same hotel room that had been so wonderfully filled with God's presence at the first celebration. This time, the celebrated son knew exactly what was coming, and he could hardly wait!

We actually arrived at the hotel before any of the other guests and were able to greet the men as they entered the room. Once again, Kathy had done a great job of decorating and had placed a beautiful cake on a table near the door. On it was the inscription "This is my beloved son, in whom I am well pleased."

Once the men arrived, we opened the celebration with a greeting and simple prayer. We followed that by singing a chorus of "Holy Spirit, Thou Art Welcome in This Place." I marveled at the fact that while not one man in the room possessed a particularly good singing voice, together we made beautiful harmony.

Two skits about emotions and the choices that men make in life followed our song. These were patterned after the lessons taught during Christopher's celebration. Next, Pastor James Glenn gave us a mini-teaching on the impact of a man's words on others. He taught us to use words to build up and never to tear down. As they were at Christopher's gathering, the messages were simple and yet profound.

Following this, we began to share our letters and gifts with Steven. Once again, I read the letters from his grandfathers and those from men far away. I must have set a record for taking the longest time to read a letter when I attempted to read my own to my son. I did quite well for a while, but when I looked up to see his face, I began to cry. I was hit with waves of wonderful thoughts about Steven, his future, his potential, and how inadequate I felt at capturing my love for him on paper.

The morning after his celebration, I reflected on the importance of a father's communicating his deepest thoughts to his son at this special time. We often don't take time to say how we really feel, and the celebration provides the perfect opportunity to bless our sons with words. Below, I have included my letter to Steven to give you some ideas about the kinds of things you may want to write to your special young man.

*To my beloved son, Steven David Molitor,
in whom I am well pleased...*

Dear Steven,

Congratulations on this special night and time of transition into manhood! During the past few years we have talked about this night, and it has finally arrived. Everything that has been done here has been done for only one purpose—to bless and support you.

The men in this room, and those who have sent greetings from far away, know how important it is for just one man to succeed in life. Their prayers and support have been with you and will continue to be with you as you walk the path of maturity.

As your father, I wanted to put some things in writing so that you would always have them. First, it's important for you to know how much I love you and how proud I am to be called your dad. As a son, you may sometimes wonder about this, especially when I get on your case about something. Rest assured, when I speak with you about anything it is to help build you into the man that God has ordained for you to become.

It has been my great pleasure to watch you grow and develop in so many areas of life. Athletics, schoolwork, music, friendships, humor, and work are all aspects of your life that impress others and me. God has given you an engineering mind that truly amazes me. You can see a project from start to finish before the first nail has been driven or shovel of dirt has been moved. When it comes time to go to work, you are on the top of my list of companions to have by my side.

God has given you a unique role to play in our family. You are often the one that gets us all going in a new direction. Your ideas are fresh and your intensity inspires others to get involved. At times, your wonderful sense of humor has turned a dull day into a complete riot. Often God has used you to lift my spirits with your fun-loving ways.

On this special night, I reflect back nearly fourteen years ago when your mother and I were in the greatest battle of our lives. You see, our precious son Steven was impatient and wanted to get on with his life right then. The problem was that he needed to stay in the womb for another six months! That was a time of incredible spiritual warfare, spiritual blessing, faith building, prayer, and weeping. Son, more than once, it looked as if we would lose you and never have the joy of your presence in our lives. It was in those times that I cried out to the Lord Jesus, who answered faithfully and brought you safely through.

I knew then that you would be a fighter in this life. I knew then that God had given you an extra measure of vitality, intensity, and zeal that few others had. God has given you these qualities to change the lives of others in positive ways. In the coming years, you will see how important your words are to others. You will see that a kind word from you can lift another up, while a harsh word from you can crush like a brick. Together, we will continue to learn how to handle this kind of power in a way that pleases God.

From early on, I also knew that God had made you a leader. This too is a quality that must be yielded to the lordship of Jesus or you will simply lead people the wrong way. I am certain that by God's grace, you will lead many into the kingdom of God, into righteousness, and into the fullness of their own callings.

One of your many gifts is found in music. You are a talented musician, but more importantly, you are an anointed one. Be careful not to allow your gift to be used by anyone other than God. God has given a similar gift to many rock musicians, rappers, and heavy metal performers—they just don't realize it, and therefore allow their gifts to be perverted. That will not happen to you. I want to encourage you to write songs that glorify God and also touch people with the beauty of life. I believe that as time passes, people throughout this land will know of your songs.

I am certain that God has written a wonderful plan for your life. It is a plan that includes honor, prosperity, family, and countless opportunities to serve him. As such, please fight against distractions and things that would steal your precious time. Time is a gift from God, and it must not be wasted. It takes hard work to live out God's calling on your life, but you can do it.

In closing, let me say that despite all of your wonderful gifts, talents, and abilities, I love you for only one reason. That is because you are my beloved son. Nothing you can do would make me love you more...or less. I am totally committed to see you through. I will never withdraw my commitment or love from you.

Son, you are about to enter into a new phase of life that will require stamina and courage. Both are within you. As you run this new race, you will sometimes have the wind at your back and the crowd cheering you on. At other times, you will feel like you can barely run another step and that everyone is against you. At those times, just keep running, Son. Never give up and never quit.

As you run, I promise that you will hear one voice cheering you on from the crowd, a voice that is different from all the rest. In that voice you will hear pride, joy, and love. Steven David, know that that voice belongs to your father.

Love,
Dad

As we had done years before, the other men then read their letters, told their stories, and blessed Steven with their gifts. Once again the range of gifts and life lessons was amazing. Steven received books, a wooden puzzle, a blessings jar, prayer journal, a candle, and many other symbolic gifts that he will treasure for a lifetime.

Once again, men sacrificed and gave away prized possessions. A beautifully designed shirt that Pastor James had brought back from a trip to Ghana became Steven's that evening. One precious brother, Teal, had recently returned from a trip to the Holy Land and gave my son a beautiful ram's-horn shofar that was over three feet in length. Teal placed the horn to his lips and blew a blast that shook the room with the sound that the warriors of old heard when it was time for battle. It was the sound that told David, Gideon, and so many others that there was an enemy on the prowl trying to take what was not theirs to take. The men in the room got the wonderfully chilling message.

As my friend blew that trumpet, I envisioned men all over the world awakening from their slumber and arming themselves for battle. As the trumpet sounded again, I could feel the war cry rising in the hearts of every man. *No longer will we allow an enemy to take our sons without a fight.* Warriors were awakened that night. We will never be caught asleep again.

When our time of letters and gifts came to a close, we brought Steven up to the front to pray blessings over him. I had some of the most senior men gather around him to pray. We prayed that God would protect, guide, and counsel this fine young man. We spoke words over Steven that every young man must hear. He heard us loudly proclaim that he is valued. He is loved. He is respected. He is accepted.

After the others had prayed, I took my place in front of my son, laid my hands upon his head, and proclaimed the essence of what the night was all about: "This is my beloved son, in whom I am well pleased."

Following this, we brought our celebration to a close and said good-bye to the many faithful men who gave up three hours of their night to bless my son for a lifetime. Kathy was waiting up for us as we arrived home, and Steven excitedly shared his experience with her. It was well into Sunday morning when the lights finally went out in our home.

DAD LEARNS HIS LESSONS TOO

Steven wasn't the only one to be blessed on that night, of course. And he certainly wasn't the only one to learn something new. In fact, I learned several new lessons from the celebration for my second son. I will use them to plan for my daughter's and my third son's celebrations, which are yet to come. I hope these lessons will assist you, as well, if you have more than one young person to celebrate.

Prepare Your Second Child for What's Ahead

Do plenty of mentoring and instructing prior to the celebration. One major difference between the celebration for my first and second son is that I had time to prepare Steven for what was going to happen. Remember that I only had three weeks from the time that I decided to hold a celebration for my first son and the event itself. This meant there were no long discussions with Christopher about the meaning of the event, his changing role in the family, the steps to maturity, and so on. I simply built upon the lessons and discussions that we'd had prior to the event and then used the celebration as a foundation for our continued mentoring.

With so little time to prepare, I decided to surprise Christopher with the event. In retrospect, I would rather not have surprised him; instead, I would have explained the scope and intent of the event to him as soon as possible. Even two weeks' notice would have been good. Fortunately, Chris's maturity level and our preexisting strong relationship made the surprise aspect of the event a nonissue.

Obviously, with Steven I had a much longer time to reflect on and then talk with him about transitional rites of passage. I strongly recommend using this reflection, discussion, and preparation model for all celebrations. However, I realize that many parents will find themselves in the same situation that I was in with my oldest son. They may not have years to prepare their boy for his transition and will simply have to start where they are in the process. Please be encouraged that it will work either way.

For those parents who have time, it's best to hold extensive discussions with your son prior to the event. Your talks should focus on the rite of passage itself and what it means for the young man's future. Clearly, these discussions are vital aspects of the event itself, even though they may take place months prior to the celebration. Fathers should be mentoring their sons all along, but especially in the months prior to their rites of passage. It will be good to talk through new expectations, changing roles, and any new responsibilities that will be given to your son.

My long-term vision is that these celebrations become part of our family culture for generations to come. Once we held Christopher's event, Kathy and I had three years to prepare for Steven's celebration, five years to prepare for Jenifer's, and seven years to prepare for Daniel's. We have used this time to have ongoing discussions about adulthood, maturity, and responsibility with each of our younger children as they eagerly anticipate their own special day of transition. As a result, the concept of rites of passage is now becoming ingrained into the very fabric of our family.

I look forward to participating in the celebrations of my children's children. The point here is that you should introduce the celebration concept to your children as soon as you possibly can so that they begin to embrace their changing roles early in life. If you missed this opportunity with your first child, then don't miss it for your second child. If you missed it for all of your children, then don't miss it for your grandchildren.

Carefully Discern the Right Time

No two sons are exactly alike. God gives us each a distinct personality, likes, and dislikes. Also, no two sons mature at exactly the same age. Your first son may be ready to accept new levels of responsibility at age thirteen while your second son may take longer to mature. There may be other factors that determine when you host your second son's celebration. If your family is going through a particularly hectic time (such as a change in location or a serious illness of a loved one) near your son's birthday, then delay his celebration for a month or two. Just let him know what is happening and why.

I decided to hold Steven's celebration approximately six months after his thirteenth birthday. At that point, his words and his actions assured me that he was ready. His maturity grew tremendously during those extra six months, and he was ready to receive the blessing of celebration.

Be Ready for the Inevitable Comparisons

Sibling rivalry is alive and well in most homes with more than one child. Mine has been no exception, and Kathy and I work very hard to ensure that none of our four offspring feels slighted, overlooked, or less valued than their siblings. Since the time of celebration is a time of powerful imprinting, it's vital that the celebration for a second or third son be of comparable size and scope as your first celebration.

Rest assured that your sons will compare notes about their respective celebrations, and there should be no glaring differences that could harm their relationship. Simply put, you would not want to host one celebration in a fancy hotel and the other in a garage. You would not want to have twenty guests at one and three at the other.

Determine the Role of the Older Brother(s)

I knew that it was important for Christopher to attend his younger sibling's celebration. I sensed that it would be a wonderful time of bonding between two brothers that sometimes viewed each other as competitors or even adversaries. Christopher wrote his own letter for his brother prior to the celebration. It was a great combination of sound advice, support, and humor. Christopher had us all laughing by pointing out that if this special event for Steven was being held in eastern Africa, we would be gathering for his circumcision. Christopher then brought the house down when he produced his gift for his brother…a razor-sharp fillet knife!

It was such a blessing to hear my oldest son read his letter and then speak from his heart. His voice was much deeper, and his words were weightier than those I had heard him utter three years earlier in this same room. His growth and maturity were evident. It made me proud to see him play such an important role in the maturing of his younger brother.

Chris knew about the importance and sanctity of the event and did nothing to trivialize the celebration in any way. During our time of prayer for Steven, Christopher came forward, placed his hands on his brother's shoulders and prayed a beautiful prayer of blessing, reconciliation, and commitment for the future. I am certain that God used that time for cleansing and strengthening the relationship between two fine young men.

THE AFTERMATH

When the celebration ended, Steven and I made the long drive home and talked about the event. He was clearly moved by the men's generosity, love, and commitment that made his celebration so special. Like his brother had done three years earlier, Steven laid his head back, closed his eyes, and quietly recounted his favorite parts of the evening. Like I had done three years earlier, I wiped tears from my eyes and thanked God for giving me a family to love.

In the days following his special night, Steven showed signs that the event had truly changed his approach to some very important aspects of life. Interestingly, he grew much closer to Daniel, his younger brother. While the two of them had been fairly close before, Steven had sometimes been antagonistic toward Daniel. Following the celebration, I watched this negative aspect of their relationship melt away. Immediately Steven was much more inclined to invite Daniel into his world and began to take on a mentor's role. Soon the two of them were engaged in work, play, and even homework projects. As a father, one of my greatest thrills is seeing my children in unity. This change in relationship between Steven and his brother has been a blessing to watch, but it did not stop there. I continue to see a similar positive change in his relationship with his other siblings as well.

Another powerful result of the celebration came when Steven made a choice to stand up for what is right under some very difficult circumstances. Several weeks after the event, he faced a tough situation at school when several of his friends became involved in some very unhealthy activities. Rather than join in, Steven confronted his peers about their actions knowing that it could cost him their companionship. I would like to report that his friends immediately saw the error of their ways, thanked Steven, and lived happily ever after, but they didn't. Instead, they withdrew and kept my son out of their lives for quite a while. I was concerned that the negative peer pressure might cause him to change his mind or soften his stand. It didn't. I am certain that Steven was emboldened by the lessons taught in the skits and strengthened by the affirmations of the men at his celebration. He still has no regrets about taking his stand despite the cost to him. I call that maturity.

A final thought on the aftermath of the celebration comes from a wonderful time Steven and I had together building his first deer-hunting blind in the woods behind our home. We spent an entire day trimming branches, hauling materials, planning, measuring, cutting, and nailing boards together. As we worked, I told my son stories about his grandfather's and great-grandfather's hunting adventures in northern Michigan. Steven was especially eager to learn more about his great-grandfather Henry, since my son inherited his love for the outdoors, hunting, and fishing.

As the day in the woods drew to a close, we put the finishing touches on our creation and then took several moments to rest inside the blind. Steven's face was beaming as he looked out of the windows at the forest glowing in all its fall brilliance. In his mind were images of a huge ten-point buck that he hoped would appear on opening day. Overhead, flocks of geese loudly announced that they were making their own rite of passage to a warmer climate.

I was soon lost in my own thoughts about the incredible beauty of God's creation and the joy of having this fine young man sit next to me in the middle of the woods. That day two men, one young and the other not so young, had worked together and built something that would last. Through the process, we laughed together, planned together, made mistakes together, and finally, as the shadows lengthened, succeeded together. At that moment, there was nowhere else on earth that I would rather have been and no one else that I would rather have had for my companion. It occurred to me that the celebration for my second son had changed my heart and made me a better dad, just as Christopher's celebration had changed me. Soon it was time to walk the winding trail back to our house. The sights, sounds, and smells of the forest surrounded us as we slowly moved toward the welcoming lights of home. Neither of us hurried or spoke much along the way. This was a day to be remembered. I had spent it with my son—my beloved son in whom I am well pleased.

CHAPTER 11

CELEBRATION FOR A WAYWARD SON

I am often asked whether parents should hold a celebration for a son who is currently rebellious or involved with drugs, alcohol, sex, violence, gangs, and so on. My response is unquestionably *yes!* I am convinced that a properly designed celebration is the key to getting many of these wayward boys back on the right path.

That is what this chapter is all about. But first we need to realistically understand the type of boy we're talking about. Then we'll consider (1) how to look past his rebellion to see something very positive, and (2) how to pay attention to what's happening in the rest of the family. Finally, I'll offer some practical suggestions to help keep hope alive in any family struggling with sons who need to change course.

LOOK REALISTICALLY AT HIS REBELLION

The term *wayward* is old-fashioned, but it still accurately describes many young males today. According to Webster, *wayward* means:

"insistent on having one's own way, contrary to others' advice, wishes, or commands; headstrong, disobedient. Conforming to no fixed rule, or pattern; unpredictable."

All too often, young men today insist on going their own way, despite the advice of those in authority. Many of the troubled youth are latchkey kids who grew up without parental supervision. Others have had fathers abandon them, leaving no positive male role model to follow. Perhaps it is easy to see why these conditions foster rebellion in young people. However, there are also many troubled, disobedient, and unpredictable teenagers who were raised in "good" homes with parents who loved them to the best of their ability. In these instances, what went wrong? I am convinced that we can find the answer here in the final line of Webster's definition, which reads "conforming to no fixed rule or pattern."

In our society, there's no shortage of rules and patterns intended to control the day-to-day behavior of our youth. Parents establish rules for when to go to sleep, timetables for when to come home on weekends, and patterns for how chores are to be done. Schools have rules about running in hallways, chewing gum, where to sit, and even when to go to the bathroom. Student athletes receive extensive coaching and instruction about particular plays or patterns in their respective sports. Coaches often have their young athletes run one play over and over again until they clearly understand how it is to be executed.

No reasonable person would challenge the notion that these kinds of rules, patterns, and intensive coaching are necessary for young people to learn basic expectations, standards, and boundaries. However, in contrast, few of our young males receive any coaching, patterns, or guidance about their impending manhood. Most simply receive a few cryptic sound bites tossed at them at random intervals. "Shape up," "be a man," and "grow up" may mean something significant to the adult saying them, but to a young person they are open to a huge variance of interpretation. While these statements are certainly not foundations upon which a young man can build his future, they are often the only ones he ever hears.

This is true even in "good" homes when the lack of a pattern for mature manhood causes young males to create their own. Sadly, their pattern is often in direct contrast to their parents' advice and wishes. The end result is waywardness, broken relationships, and damaged lives. Yet even this can be turned around.

In Luke 15:11-32, we read a fascinating story involving a father and his two sons. The older son is a real gem. We learn from the account that he is obedient and respectful of his father. He seems to have a real sense of purpose for his life as he diligently stays at home to take care of the family business, which someday he will inherit.

His younger brother is exactly the opposite. Brash, shortsighted, and demanding, this rebellious son prematurely takes his share of their father's estate and heads off to a distant country, where he squanders both his money and his self-respect. He enjoys the temporary pleasures of sin in the company of prostitutes but soon ends up at his life's lowest point.

Eventually, this wayward son comes to his senses and chooses to return home, where his father holds a wonderful celebration in his honor. The father proudly announces the reason for the celebration to those in attendance: His son was dead and now is alive, his son was lost and now he is found! To any father, this is a great reason to celebrate!

As I study this ancient passage, it is clear that its primary message is about the unconditional love that our heavenly Father has for lost souls. However, I'm also amazed at its many implications for the celebration concept today if we view the account simply as a story about an earthly father and his two sons. Seen from this perspective, we learn:

Modern-Day Teen Rebellion Is Nothing New

Young males have been making bad decisions with their lives for generations. Also, it is clear that the traps for our young people today are no different than they were back then. Drunkenness, rebellion against authority, and sexual immorality are still high on the list of common snares for unsuspecting young men.

Teen Rebellion Has a Wide Impact

Another interesting aspect of the account is that not only are the traps the same, but so is the impact of teen rebellion on everyone involved. Parents of wayward sons are devastated and distracted from the other aspects of their own lives. Siblings are torn: They love their brothers but also harbor resentment over what seems like unfair tolerance of their poor behavior.

Teen Rebellion Hurts…Teens

We tend to forget that the worst impact of the rebellion is always inflicted upon the teens themselves. They suffer spiritually, physically, financially, mentally, emotionally, and relationally as wild living robs their vitality and their zeal for life. In getting what they thought they wanted, these wayward souls actually lose what they so desperately need—structure, family unity, boundaries, purpose, and direction. They pay a heavy price for gaining too much freedom too soon.

Yet all is not lost. We can approach the wayward son from a hopeful perspective by learning to look at him in a new way.

LOOK PAST THE REBELLION

The good news about this story is it reminds us that despite all of our youthful mistakes, there comes a time when even the most rebellious young man comes to his senses and wants to return to home base for another try at life. This should give hope to so many parents whose boys have chosen the wayward road. Please don't give up. Keep watching down the road for their return. And keep in mind that in the story we see two key people in this reconciliation process: the father and the son. When the dad saw his son, he seemingly had every right to go down the road and angrily berate him with several years' worth of "I told you this would happen!" He did not do this.

Instead, he saw his wayward son when he was *still far away* and ran to him, kissed him, and honored him with a robe and special ring of authority. This is a model for all of us to follow. Can you picture how the boy looked after his long time of wild living, poverty, and filth? Can you imagine how the boy smelled after literally living with pigs? And yet the father ran to him and kissed him.

Clearly, the father saw what others missed when they looked at this wayward son. As only a parent can, this father *looked past the filth and saw all of the potential,* the promise, the gifts, and the calling that a sovereign God had placed within his boy. With sadness he saw the lines around his young man's eyes and the scars on his body that inevitably come from a hard life on the road. However, despite the scars, he knew that there was once again hope for this young man's future. This was well worth celebrating!

ATTEND TO THE FAMILY IMPACT

Jesus uses this parable to tell us about God's love for us even when we are lost and destitute. Again, let's consider the story from a different angle as well, using the story as a springboard for the topic of this book by putting an earthly father in the place of God the Father in the parable.

It is difficult to imagine the emotional highs and lows experienced by the father that day. Shortly after the thrill of seeing his young son return, the father found himself confronted by a very angry older son who told him, "Look! All these years I've been slaving for you and never disobeyed your orders.... But when this son of yours who has squandered your property with prostitutes comes home, you kill the fattened calf for him!" (Luke 15:29-30). The wayward son's rebellion had an impact on the family that couldn't be ignored.

At first glance, the older son's words seem to indicate a resentment of his sibling's party. I have heard numerous well-meaning preachers condemn the older brother's response as jealous and envious. They seem to ignore that the older brother did have plenty of reasons to be upset—they didn't even come to get him when the party started! But in fact the older brother never said that his brother's return should be ignored or that his homecoming was not a legitimate cause for celebration. The older son simply spoke his mind about his father's lack of celebration of *his* life. Perhaps the events of the day helped identify what had quietly troubled him for years. His message to his father declares: "Dad, for years now you have watched me grow, trusted me with the family fortune, and prepared me to rule over this estate someday. All this, and yet you failed to acknowledge my accomplishments, manhood, and maturity with even a modest celebration. That hurts!"

I find it fascinating that while the older brother had everything money could buy, including houses, lands, servants, and livestock, he was troubled by what he did *not* have—a celebration initiated by his father. Imagine the impact on this family if the story had been written something like this:

> A man had two sons. When his older son came of age, the father decided to hold a special celebration to acknowledge his manhood, clarify his identity, and launch him on the journey to maturity.
>
> While the younger son was still at home the father ran to him and hugged him. He then called his servants and friends to gather for a celebration in his son's honor, just as he had done for his elder son several years earlier.
>
> At the celebration, his father had a feast prepared of his son's favorite foods. After the dinner, he placed a handsome cloak over this son's shoulders to signify that a new mantle of manhood had arrived. He then placed a special ring of authority on his son's finger.
>
> During the celebration, the father shared with his son about the many wonderful opportunities that

awaited him in life. Also, he encouraged his son to demonstrate increasing maturity as he waited to receive his full inheritance. Then some of the men in attendance told the young man of their tragic journeys to distant lands that had beckoned them with promises of sexual pleasures, lavish parties, and the lure of unlimited freedom.

They told the young man of the dangers of his following this path and how they themselves eventually returned home muddied and bloodied, having to start over again. They told him of a better path that would leave him safe and satisfied. Other friends told him of the blessings of obedience, patience, and self-control.

The father and his friends then blessed the son with many prayers, gifts, and affirmations of his true identity. After their time of celebration ended, the father and his two sons went about their lives until it was time to celebrate the coming of age of their next generation.

As much as I honor the inspired biblical account about our heavenly Father's compassion, I like to envision the story with an earthly father and his two sons played out in the manner above. While the ending seems much the same, the second account eliminates all doubt about the father's love and the devastating effects of waywardness on everyone involved. When we learn to celebrate our sons *before* they head off to distant lands, we will all benefit greatly. This is a lesson for every parent whose son is still living at home. Don't wait!

KEEP HOPE ALIVE!

Of course, many parents have sons who have already departed, either physically or emotionally. Often, parents of these wayward ones feel that all they can do is wait for their son to reappear. While these seem like the bleakest times, there are several reasons to remain hopeful. First, your heavenly Father loves your son more than you do. Your son is first and foremost a creation of God and therefore, despite his waywardness, he will always have his heavenly Father's attention.

Second, even if your son has gone to a distant land, you can still reach him with prayer. "Watch and pray" is a much better strategy than "watch and worry." Sooner or later, you will see him coming down the road. Don't stop watching and don't stop praying.

Third, each of us was created with a desire to know who we are, where we are from, and why we are here. No one ever found his true identity in wayward living, and no one ever puts down lasting roots in a sin-filled life. Eventually, like the younger son in the parable, your son will desire to reconnect with his family. When this happens, don't ask questions. Just run to him, hug him, and plan his celebration.

Remember, the father in the biblical account held the celebration for his son when his boy was still filthy and before there was any proof that he had truly changed. If you wait to hold a celebration for your son until he has his life totally together, you will never hold one. Again, why wait?

Without question, a celebration itself is the key to much of your boy's future. Perhaps for the first time in his life, he will be honored just for being a man. With his harsh life experiences as a backdrop, a wayward son is able to understand the two basic paths that every man has before him. One path leads toward maturity, responsibility, and lasting satisfaction. The other leads toward immaturity, irresponsibility, temporary pleasures, and lasting regret. He will appreciate another chance to try the right path.

If you are able to contact your son, then go to him. Attempt to reconcile the differences you may have and begin to rebuild your relationship. Forgive him now for whatever grief or embarrassment he has caused you. Our society has made it easy to divorce our spouses, but fortunately it has not yet figured out a way for us to divorce our children. He is still your son!

As a father, you must accept and remember that God gave your son to you and no amount of family conflict will ever change that. If out-of-sight becomes out-of-mind, your mind is on too many other things that are not nearly as important as your son.

Please don't think I'm being insensitive to the nearly unbearable grief that our sons can bring into our lives with wrong choices. Over the years, I have worked in prisons and with programs for troubled youth, and have heard every imaginable horror story about family breakdown. I have held far too many parents in my arms as they wept for their wayward sons. These were not sons who simply ran away from home. Many were sons who cursed, mocked, stole from, shamed, and physically hurt their parents. Often, these young men ended up in jails, prisons, or other detention programs, seemingly out of reach. However, I am certain that our heavenly Father is able to touch a son in the darkest place on earth and break through to even the hardest heart. The bond that holds fathers and sons together is never broken to the point where God cannot reconstruct it.

Just as I have seen the many tragedies, I have also seen a large number of miracles that reunited families and got young men back on the road to mature manhood. As expected, there is a pattern to this process of reconciliation. Prayer is the foundation, and unconditional love is the motive. You must love your son despite what he has done. This never means that you love his sin, but rather that his sin has not caused you to stop loving *him*. Forgiveness is essential. Without it, you will simply become a ticking time bomb, waiting to explode about your son's past transgressions at the worst possible time.

Finally, you'll need to be patient if you're to avoid countless sleepless nights. Remember the father who watched for his son to come down the road and saw him when he was far off. My guess is the father looked in the daylight and slept at night. Keep the rest of your life moving forward as you patiently wait. Keep watching, praying, and loving. Pour out your love and attention on the family members that remain. When your son does come back, *immediately* make your plans for the celebration that will launch him forward on his journey to mature manhood.

PRACTICAL SUGGESTIONS

Here are some thoughts and suggestions to help you plan a celebration for your son.

Recognize How Much Your Son Has Already Changed
Understand that a young man who has lived waywardly for any length of time is quite different now. Sadly, he is not the same little boy he was before. Like Adam after the fall, his eyes may have been opened to things that he was never created to see. His mind may be filled with

what was previously unthinkable. Drugs, sex, drunkenness, crime, rejection, and violence all cause deep wounds in a young man's soul. They may cloud his view of even the most sincere efforts to help him regain his spiritual and relational footing.

This simply means that you may not get the reaction you are looking for when the concept of celebration is first announced to him. Remain patient. The celebration is the right thing to do, regardless of his initial reaction. The wayward son may look disinterested in the letters and gifts that are brought to him on his special night. However, as time passes, these will be treasured keepsakes that God will use to encourage him when no one else is looking.

Avoid a Big Surprise

I would not recommend that you surprise a wayward son with a celebration. My inclination is to let him know well beforehand that you have a gathering planned in his honor so he can adjust to the concept. He will probably think long and hard about it. A surprise may be too much for him to handle emotionally and could make him feel very uncomfortable.

Invite Just the Right Men

When planning a celebration for a wayward son, I would also prayerfully consider who to invite and, just as important, who *not* to invite. You do not need a friend or relative using the celebration as an opportunity to "set your boy straight."

Quite frankly, the celebration isn't the time to push hard for your son's conversion to an active life of faith or to drag him back into the mainstream of society. Instead, it is time to demonstrate your love for him and to show that a different way of life exists. It is time to tell him truths about his own manhood, show that a good path still lies ahead, and lovingly encourage him to make good choices. The celebration is time to confirm and affirm that he is a man. It is a time for other men to talk about some of their own mistakes from the past and share how God helped get them back on track.

Recall the Good Times

The celebration for a wayward son is also a time to rekindle good memories from the past. I realize that you may have to go back years to remember a time when your relationship consisted of more than shouting matches and slamming doors followed by long periods of silence. However, nearly every family has some special moments buried in the past. It may be a fishing trip or vacation that occurred more than a decade ago. It may be just a quiet moment spent together on a couch. Perhaps a father and son took a long drive and talked about life. The boy's first hit in baseball or his first basket may be a milestone worth revisiting. Your son's talent as a carpenter, artist, singer, and so on are positive things to be remembered. You may want to show him an old videotape or photo album of his childhood. These flashbacks to the past will help him to know that his life has not been all bad; he once knew happier times.

Regardless of what your son has experienced during his time of waywardness, know that God has made sure that some good memories are safely stored inside his mind and will reappear with just a gentle nudge. Your job is to lovingly wake him from the temporary "amnesia" that seems to afflict so many wayward boys. No amount of shouting, threatening, or intimidation ever helped someone regain their footing and/or sense of true identity. That takes love, patience, and a series of gentle reminders of who they truly are. One of the most crucial messages for you to share when your son comes back is that God is able to create a new beginning for any man who has the courage to ask him for it. He has not gone too far for God to restore. You must give him sufficient hope to overcome the feelings of loss, shame, guilt, and hopelessness that often walk alongside a boy returning home from his time of waywardness.

Make the Format a Good Fit

I'd be careful not to do skits or dramas that could be interpreted as condemning any of your son's previous mistakes. In fact, skits should be designed to focus on the positive aspects of life and the benefits of mature manhood. If some appropriate humor can be added to keep things relaxed, that would be good—as long as it does not trivialize the event.

One of the most important aspects of the celebration, especially for a wayward son, is for you to pray and speak blessings over him. Wayward boys have heard plenty of curses. They need to hear blessings! They need to hear words of hope and a future. You can provide these life-giving words.

Also, your son needs to hear you and the other men in attendance say that he is unconditionally accepted, no matter how wayward he has been. It is vital that you communicate that the God who created him to do great things is always waiting for the slightest sign that the boy is coming home—just like the father in the biblical account.

Keep an Open Mind About the Response

I want to encourage you parents to prepare for and host your son's celebration without prejudging how he, or you, will respond. Let's start with you. Be prepared for some emotions to be stirred and some tears to flow. If you are angry with your son, then get prayer or counseling before the celebration so that you are able to truly be a blessing to him at this crucial time.

On the day of his celebration, it is difficult to predict how your son will react. He may seem upbeat and happy, or he may appear sullen, depressed, or disinterested.

It may seem simplistic to say that every wayward son will respond either positively or negatively to his celebration. But, remember, these young men have been living a life of extremes. Some of them may become angry because the celebration is showing them what they've been missing. If they feel too "dirty" to accept the unconditional love offered, they may aggressively reject it. Others may think it's too late for their lives to change. For example, the young man who is in a gang may feel that he would put his family in danger if he leaves the gang, so he feels trapped in his destructive lifestyle. Be ready for many of these possible responses.

It is good to keep in mind that a celebration is the door to maturity, not the final destination. Some boys may respond positively to the celebration—perhaps breaking down in tears—but have no idea how to go about changing. They may need many more months or years before they can truly incorporate what it all means into their lives.

Regardless of the initial emotions displayed on his special evening, your son's life will probably move in one of two essential directions. The first possibility is that he will immediately recognize a better way to live, run to you, ask for forgiveness, and you will move on with life together. The celebration will be the key to returning him to his family, society, and the path the God has for his life. If that happens, it will be wonderful, and I have no doubt that many families will see this occur.

However, a second possibility is that your son will not immediately turn his life around. There may not be an instant rekindling of love between father and son. Please remember that the cycle of sin, guilt, and shame often causes boys to bury their emotions so that no one sees inside them. If this happens, don't despair or accept the lie that the celebration somehow failed. You have planted some wonderful seeds that will grow within your son. In time, they will bring forth a harvest of maturity.

Even if things seem to worsen after the celebration, you have released the incredible power of a blessing. The celebration will remain an unmistakable sign of your devotion to your son that can never be taken away. God will cause the event to act like a wonderful flower that grows in your son's soul at just the right time.

Regardless of which immediate reaction you get from your son, you will have done the right thing for the right reason. Following the event, if you must wait a little longer for your son to completely return to his senses, this will make your wait much easier. The only way that a celebration for your son will fail is if you fail to hold one!

CHAPTER 12

CELEBRATIONS FOR ALL FAMILY STRUCTURES

Not every child grows up in a home with both a mother and a father. Death, divorce, absenteeism, and abuse are sad realities of today's society. Sociologists, counselors, and psychologists have put forth a steady stream of theories on how to help children adjust to the realities of a home with only one parent. While many books have been written on the impact of divorce or a parent's death, there is one aspect that has been largely overlooked: the transition of our young people into adulthood.

CELEBRATIONS IN CHAOS?

When divorce or a parent's death occurs in the first ten to fifteen years of marriage, young children or teenagers are often involved. In the case of divorce, children must adjust to divided loyalties and often bitter battles for affection. Regardless of how the home became a single-parent home, the mother or father each faces new struggles of their own. They must adjust to changes in their finances, location, responsibilities, and schedules. Things change socially for them as well. Often, dating begins again. New people appear on the scene and must be factored into family life. As all of this change swirls around single parents, most do their best to make sure that their children have the essentials they need—food, shelter, education, and support. For all involved, life begins to move rapidly forward as they try to adjust to the new realities.

Somewhere in this blur of chaotic change, there is one constant. The children are growing, one day at a time, toward their own adulthood. This fact is often overlooked, with serious consequences. Granted, single parents with barely enough time for themselves watch for signs of trouble with their displaced children. They do the best they can with obvious problems that arise, but they may mistakenly believe that if their child shows no outward sign of trouble, then they are fine on the inside as well.

Obviously, it's great when a young person survives the early years of a single-parent home without any major problems with substance abuse or legal trouble. Many of them do. However, so much attention has been placed on simply surviving the ordeal that the child's need for help in making the transition into adulthood is ignored. Regardless of how stoic a child appears, his internal struggle with identity and adulthood still simmers. This is why single parents must understand the importance of rights of passage for their children.

Another single-parent scenario should be mentioned here: Many children today are born to unwed mothers. In these instances, there is no divorce or death for the child to contend with. Instead, there is simply a void in his life where his father should be. The son grows up in a world devoid of a consistent male role model and, because he doesn't consciously miss what he never had, may seem better adjusted than his friends with divorced parents.

Whether a child is born out of wedlock or loses his family structure as a result of divorce or death, he will desperately need someone to help launch him on his personal journey to maturity. Love, support, mentoring, and a listening ear are all essential for his proper development. However, he needs more than that. Each child, especially those without one or both parents, must have help making the transition into adulthood.

A rite of passage will bring much-needed stability and new hope to each young celebrant. I am firmly convinced that the celebration will help set new standards for love, commitment, and wise choices that will serve the young person well as he builds his own family in the coming years. Here is how it can work for you.

GEARING UP FOR SINGLE-FATHER CELEBRATIONS

Of course, a single parent can be either a mom or a dad. In terms of a celebration, the single dad will have fewer modifications to make in the planning process. A single father can essentially follow the same pattern outlined in this book with one modification. If the father has never really talked about the divorce or loss with his son, then he should do so prior to the celebration.

I must be clear here that if divorce is involved, the purpose of the sharing is not to discredit the boy's mother or to point out her faults. It is not a time to criticize or scandalize in-laws, lawyers, or other outsiders. Instead, it is time to talk about the pain of divorce and the problems it causes for every member of a family. Remember, whatever we grow up with is "normal." If a boy grows up in a divided home, then for him that is the pattern for a family. Prior to the celebration, the father would want to share God's lifelong plan for marriage, family, and child rearing.

Your son should enter into manhood with a clear understanding of the foundations for a healthy family. Perhaps later, father and son can discuss details of what went wrong for mom and dad. For now he simply needs to know that he does not have to follow the same pattern that more than 50 percent of couples do when it comes to marriage and child rearing. The conversations that happen just before, during, and after the celebration will stick with your son for a lifetime. Choose your words carefully.

If the boy's mother still has some connection with the family, it is crucial that she be kept informed about the plans for two reasons. First, so that she does not schedule a conflicting event on the same date as your son's celebration. Second, and more important, so that she can be part of the process. This is a time for some real humility and personal sacrifice for moms and dads who have gone their separate ways.

When a relationship is broken, of course, feelings are hurt. Divorce often results in bitterness, resentment, and a "get even" mentality. If there were ever a time for a man and woman to set these negatives aside and work together, it is now. Their son's future is worth far more than either parent's ego and will be influenced by the cooperation, or lack thereof, that he sees during this special time. The foundational thought here is that the single father should inform the boy's mother of his intent and include her in appropriate ways before and after the celebration. Once this issue is covered, the father simply designs and hosts his son's celebration as I've laid out in previous chapters.

DEFINING THE ROLE OF SINGLE MOTHERS

More often than not, the single parent is the mother, which creates some unique circumstances for her son's celebration. Can she still create a celebration for her son? Definitely! In fact, it is crucial that she help provide her son with what other men in her life may have lacked—a transition into manhood.

As hard as it may be for a single mom to accept, there is one primary difference between her and a single male parent when it comes to celebrations for her son: Mom must not be the one to host her son's celebration. For years she may have been both father and mother to her son. She may have worked both inside and outside the home just to make ends meet. She may have provided strength, nurturing, love, and discipline for her son without much help from anyone else. However, despite all of these wonderful acts of love, service, and sacrifice, there is one thing that she can never be: a model of manhood.

It is for this reason that I strongly recommend that single moms resist the temptation to host the celebrations themselves. This is a time when she must make a transition herself concerning her son. She must be willing to temporarily let go of her boy and allow him to become a man in the presence of other men. Although it is not the primary focus of the event, a rite of passage helps young males establish new relationships with their mothers and other women in their lives. While this new relationship involves a momentary separation from mom, it will result in a lifetime of respect and admiration for her many acts of kindness and sacrifice on his behalf.

The proper way forward is for the single mother to enlist at least one adult male whom she respects and trusts as the overseer of the celebration. This may be her pastor, priest, male relative, and/or an appropriate man from her local church, scout group, or other similar organization. It is important to find a mature man to lead the ceremony. His organizational skills will make the planning easier, and his presence at the celebration will be the foundation for the whole process. Ideally, it will be someone respected by her son and someone who can have ongoing contact with him after the celebration is completed.

But I have some warnings here. In order to prevent any tragedies with the celebration, allow me to be straightforward about two issues:

Issue #1: No Temporary Boyfriends

First, I need to underscore that the man called upon to host the celebration should not be mom's temporary boyfriend, who may not be around in a few months. It is a fact of life that men and women begin dating again after a divorce or death of a spouse. Obviously, this complicated process does not go unnoticed by the children.

To be fair, sometimes mom's serious boyfriend (or dad's serious girlfriend) can bring much needed support and stability to the family that has survived an abusive spouse. When this is the case, the young people involved will eventually recognize that fact. However, children of divorce often view these new people as competition for their parent's affection, as the cause of the divorce itself, or at least as a stumbling block to their parents' reconciliation. In these instances, it would be a huge mistake for a single mom to expect her new boyfriend to successfully host a celebration for her son.

One idea would be for the boyfriend to write a letter to the son and give it to him *after* the celebration has concluded. This way, if the man becomes a permanent part of the son's life, he will have had a tangential role in the celebration. If the new boyfriend eventually departs from the scene, no harm will have been done.

Issue #2: Check on Backgrounds

A single mom may let other people know of her search to find an adult male to assist with her son's celebration and journey to mature manhood. She may share her need with her relatives, neighbors, members of her congregation, or her coworkers. So far, there is nothing wrong with this process. However, when she has one or more volunteers for the celebration, she must carefully check these men out to determine their motives and their backgrounds.

It is a sad commentary on today's society that some sick men join certain organizations just so that they can get close to young males. My strongest recommendation is that moms don't automatically assume that because someone came forth to volunteer, he is the right man for the job. Check the person's background; get character references from someone you know. Ask questions.

Don't worry about offending the man. Be assured that the right man will not have a problem with your efforts to protect your son. If a prospective host does object to your inquisitions, cross him off your list and move on. If you are not comfortable that you have found a suitable candidate to host your son's celebration, then simply wait, watch, and pray until the right person comes forth. It is better to delay the event for a few weeks or even months than to open the door to more heartache.

Selecting a Spiritual Man

One of the most vital considerations for deciding which man to select involves the issue of spirituality. In a world filled with so many different ideas about religion, a mom must really understand a prospective host's views on the subject.

Don't assume that someone shares your faith, even if he attends the same church as you do. Make sure! This is vital in today's bizarre world where what was once considered lunacy has now become the norm. In a society where to call anything *sin* is seen as intolerant and politically incorrect, it would be dangerous to assume anything about another person's actual spiritual beliefs.

Select a man whose approach to spirituality is acceptable to you and in line with your approach to your faith. Make sure that the individual has found answers to his own questions about God before you put him in charge of your son's special event. The last thing a boy needs on his special night is for his host to send confusing signals about faith and spirituality.

A good approach here is for the mother to meet with the prospective host for an initial discussion. They could talk about the celebration process and have a frank discussion of what will be communicated about spirituality. If you are uncomfortable with the man's approach, continue your search until you find a suitable host. One will become available if you do not give up! God has blessed men throughout the world with a true father's anointing. These are not men who would schedule your son's special event as if it were just another meeting. Instead, the right man will prayerfully prepare for the celebration as if it were one of the most important days of his *own* life.

It is an honor to be chosen to help a young person transition into adulthood. When you find a man who understands this truth, sign him up. Not only will he do a complete job of planning and hosting the event, he will also be the proper man to pray over your son at the conclusion.

Once the right man is located, and when he agrees to accept responsibility for overseeing the event, the mom can assist him in all phases of the preparation. This will include providing a list of grandfathers, uncles, brothers, family friends, and other possible attendees along with their names and contact information.

As the planning process moves forward, the mother can again meet with the host and give him some background about her son. This includes her son's vision, his passion, his favorite activities, his fears, and his greatest challenges in life. Armed with this information, the host can focus on the most important issues and avoid any highly sensitive subjects.

Once the single mom has made a "handoff" to a qualified adult male, she can prayerfully wait for her son's special day to arrive. During this time, she can counsel her son about the changes that are coming and assure him that her love for him will never fade, even after he has become a man.

PLANNING CELEBRATIONS BY GRANDPARENTS

In the past few months, I've had the pleasure of helping two grandfathers design unique celebrations for their teenaged grandsons. Each of them did so under heartbreaking circumstances. In the first situation, the boy's father had murdered his mother and was placed in prison for life. In a split second, the boy had lost both parents. In the second situation, the boy's father had committed suicide, leaving the boy and his mother to face the challenges of life alone. Fortunately for those who were left to cope with the unimaginable, the grandfathers decided to intervene and create powerful celebrations for their grief-stricken grandsons. In both cases, the grandfathers reported that the impact of the celebration on the boys was profound. It was as if a wall of protection was built between them and the tragedies of their recent pasts.

Grandparents can create and host celebrations for their grandsons by following the steps outlined in this book. They must remember that it is never appropriate to criticize another family member at a celebration. Further, it would be wrong to belittle an absentee or unfit parent in front of the young man. This means that no matter how angry you are at a son-in-law or daughter-in-law, you must not vent any of that anger during your grandson's special event. Remember that the focus of the celebration is on his future, not your past.

I am convinced that grandparents are extremely effective hosts for celebrations, even when parents are less-than-ideal role models for their sons. If a boy's parents don't wish to hold a celebration for their son, a grandfather can still ask for permission to host the event. The grandfather can use the event to bestow powerful second-generation blessings upon his heritage and launch the boy on his journey to mature manhood.

CELEBRATIONS FOR YOUNG MEN OUTSIDE YOUR FAMILY

In 1999 I held a unique celebration for a wonderful young man named Brian Pruitt. It was unique for two reasons. First, it was held for a nonfamily member and, second, the celebrant was nearly thirty years old at the time.

I first met Brian when he arrived some years before at the church I attend. Over time, I had come to view him as part of my family. At the time of his celebration, Brian was married to his beautiful wife, Dede, and was serving as a youth pastor in a church in Detroit.

In the time I have known him, Brian has always had a lot going for him. An incredible athlete, Brian played football at Central Michigan University until he graduated in 1994. In his senior year he was the second leading rusher in the nation and was named a first-team all-American. As a result, the young man was on the Bob Hope college football television special and played in numerous college bowl games. The story of his accomplishments made headlines throughout the country. However, what the headlines did not tell was that one of Brian's greatest victories was surviving his boyhood on the streets of Saginaw, Michigan, without a father. With the loving support of his mother, some coaches, and older family members, Brian made it through a turbulent childhood and began to excel in athletics.

During his college years, Brian spent many hours at my home playing with my children, eating at our table, and talking with us about his life. During those times, I could see that despite all the awards and adulation, there was something missing. After I held the first celebration for my son, Christopher, I became burdened with the need to help put back what life without a full-time father had taken from Brian.

One fall day in 1999, I invited about a dozen men to come to my home to celebrate Brian Pruitt's life and to affirm his manhood. It was a marvelous gathering that resulted in a tremendous blessing for all of us—especially for Brian.

I am always amazed at the wonderful presence of God that fills the room whenever men gather to celebrate another man's identity. Brian's event was no exception. The rest of us assembled prior to Brian's arrival. Here were twelve men sitting around talking about the weather, the football scores, our families, and many other topics not related to the celebration. As soon as Brian arrived, we turned our attention to him and could literally feel a wonderful change in the room. The men got very quiet as someone said an opening prayer. Then, as with my son's celebration, some amazing things began to happen.

The first activity was to pass around a piece of paper with Brian's name at the top. We asked the attendees to write down the first two words that came to their minds when they thought about Brian. The paper quickly made the rounds and returned to me. I slowly read the words that captured the essence of the man:

"Leader...Friend...Man of God...Integrity...Courageous."

By the time I finished reading the last word, tears had begun to flow from our eyes. Next, we read letters that the men had brought with them for Brian. Life lessons, personal victories, and deep heartaches all poured forth with great power. Brian sat very still as he listened to his friends talk about their lives, their families, and their God.

One young man in attendance was only sixteen at the time. Over the past few years, he had gotten to know Brian through church activities. It was clear that this young man had watched with admiration as Brian handled all of the pressures of stardom and still maintained his integrity and his faith. The young man was facing slightly away from Brian when it came time to share his letter. As he began to read, he turned to glance at Brian's face. As soon as their eyes met, the young man burst into tears. His letter dropped to the floor as he told of all the respect for Brian that had been stored in his heart. It was an amazing testimony of the impact of one man's life on another.

We finished our celebration with Brian by praying a blessing over him and sending him home with many gifts and symbols of our love for him.

In your own life, you probably know young men who were raised under tough circumstances. Divorce, absentee parents, death, abuse, the list goes on. Whether the path they are currently on seems good or bad, it will get infinitely better when someone takes the initiative to celebrate the seeds of greatness residing in those young men. The time and effort that it takes are insignificant when compared with the incredible benefits that will be realized when you celebrate the life of another. As you've read this chapter, has anyone come to mind? A young man who needs to have his life, manhood, and identity celebrated?

If so, don't wait. Get planning now!

CHAPTER 13

IS YOUR CHURCH
CARING FOR
YOUNG MEN?

Today's world is filled with thousands of differing religious practices. They range all the way from the mundane to the bizarre. Even within the Christian church, there is a wide variety of religious expression and doctrine. One group dances with rattlesnakes to prove their faith while another concludes that a single hand raised in praise is decidedly *un*religious. With these differing practices in mind, I am glad that God spoke to one of the early disciples about the subject of true religion. Reading James 1:27 should bring us back to our senses—at least for a moment: "Religion that God our Father accepts as pure and faultless is this: to look after orphans and widows in their distress and to keep oneself from being polluted by the world."

James 1:27 is an extremely powerful passage, and the idea of looking after orphans has strong implications for the celebration of manhood. Let's look a little closer at this concept.

Care for the Fatherless

To better understand this passage in James, we need to look deeper into what God means by "look after" here. And whom did he have in mind when he said "orphans"? In the original Greek language of the New Testament, the word for orphan is *orphanos*. This word means "comfortless" and "fatherless."

To "look after" is a translation of the Bible's Greek word *episkeptomai*. It is used in the active sense and means "to look upon something with mercy and favor; to take care of; to go and visit." Now, if you will allow me to put these concepts together and just focus on the issue of orphans, the passage could accurately read like this: "Religious practices that God our Father accepts as pure and faultless are these: To look with mercy and favor upon the fatherless children who are currently without comfort. Also, to not only look upon them, but to go and visit them and to take care of them as a loving father would."

The implications of this passage for Christian men are staggering. It convicts me of having a mind-set about church and ministry that is completely opposite from God's. How many times have I hurried past the Sunday school classrooms filled with young people, never once stopping to consider their needs? I was in too much of a hurry to get into the service (think about the word *service* for a moment) so that I could let God know how much I love him. Amazingly, God tells us that if we want to show him that we love him, then we are to look after the fatherless.

There are two types of fatherless youth in our churches today. The first literally have no father in the home. Dad has either died or departed. Other fatherless children have a male who lives under the same roof but either abuses or neglects his children.

In recent years, many different groups have established programs to help meet the needs of the fatherless. Government agencies, public schools, and privately funded organizations have done what they could to touch our troubled youth. Many churches have also made youth services a vital part of their ministries. Often, these innovative churches have bus or van ministries. This means that they send vehicles into their communities to pick up young people who otherwise would not be able to attend services. After the service (there is that word again!) is over, the youth are driven home, back to the same environment that they left a few hours before. A week later, the cycle repeats itself.

These few hours each week give these "orphans" hope that there are people who care about them and that life has some ups to accompany the downs. The church is the ideal place for these young people not only to receive spiritual instruction, but also to find a surrogate father to celebrate them into manhood.

God himself has put together the church to do more than sing a few hymns and build buildings. Within each local church exists both parts of the equation needed to rebuild an entire community, nation, and world. In one room sit hungry, hurting youth, waiting for someone to show them the way forward. In another room sit men who are successfully making their way through the minefield of life. These men may or may not have official church titles such as pastor or elder; however, they are specially equipped to serve those young people so dear to God's heart.

It's a Matter of Service

I've asked you to think about the word *service*. The point is this: I strongly suggest that each church revisit its mission and how it approaches service to its youth. Why not try something radically different? Refuse to accept the idea that any of the young people who walk through the doors ever have to fall. It is a matter of aligning the church's vision with God's clearly stated purpose and then connecting hurting youth with loving father figures who will care for, look after, and comfort them.

Each church should implement a mentoring relationship among its men and the young people it serves. The program can be something as simple as assigning each interested man one or two young people whom he greets and prays for each week. It can then progress into a mentoring relationship where the young man is invited to participate in some of his mentor's family events. Over time, trusting relationships between the men and the young people will develop. As these youth come of age, a celebration can be planned for each of them and implemented at the church or at the mentor's home. The impact on the young people, the mentor, the church, and society will be life-changing.

Obviously, every attempt should be made to involve the young person's natural family members if they are willing. This will open up another great door of ministry to the boy's family as his mentor calls or visits his home. Chances are good that those at home have never experienced someone's showing unconditional love and concern for them. Their initial reaction may be one of skepticism, but given enough time such attitudes will turn to gratitude.

The men of the church can help each other host celebrations for their young partners by following the guidelines in this book. In time, some of the same young men who were initially mentored will return to take their place as mentors to the next generation of "orphans."

I realize that some pastors, especially youth pastors, may read about this concept with some frustration. Often, they either don't have enough men in their congregations to go around or, sadly, the men who are available simply won't commit to this type of service. There are still some powerful ways to bless the young people in the church, though.

Ideally the pastor will hold a celebration for each of the fatherless youth who attend his church. Clearly, this involves a lot of work, but what other investment offers a better return than time and energy poured into the lives of our young people? If the boy's mother or guardian is open to the idea, the pastor can make all the necessary arrangements to host the event right at the church. He can then invite members of the staff, along with a few other men from the congregation, to attend and help the event succeed.

If a lot of young people attend the church, or if time is a primary concern, the pastor could host a celebration for more than one young man simultaneously. The main components of the celebration will still be very similar to the one described in this book. Perhaps the primary difference is that adult attendees would need to bring multiple letters and gifts. Done in this manner, the celebration(s) may take a bit longer to complete, but it will be time well spent. An additional benefit of this approach is that some deep bonding will take place among the celebrants as they enter into manhood together.

With all of the possible variations, there are many unique ways to put a celebration together. Recently I was invited to help design and participate in an interesting church-sponsored celebration. An internationally known evangelist came to minister in our area and brought his family with him. For years, this man had dedicated his life to missionary outreaches in Third-World countries. My private conversation with him revealed that he was often torn between the needs of his family and the demands of his ministry. As he shared from his heart, he told of his great love for his teenage son, who often accompanied him on his trips abroad. His son was going to turn sixteen during the week that he was in our area, and this preacher knew that he needed to do something special for him. He just wasn't sure what it should be.

When a friend and I shared the celebration concept with him, the evangelist was overjoyed. The challenge was that he and his son would be in town only a few more days. After a mad scramble of phone calls, room reservations, skit creation, and invitations to prospective male attendees, we had the basics pulled together.

Two nights later, we had assembled twelve men in the downstairs fellowship hall of the church and waited for the evangelist to finish his ministry in the sanctuary upstairs. At about nine o'clock, he led his son downstairs under the guise of getting some refreshments. The young man's eyes grew wide when he saw the men assembled and learned that the celebration was in his honor. After an opening prayer, we presented several skits about integrity, manhood, and the need for a man to leave behind childish things as he pursues maturity. Some of the skits were very solemn and others were hilarious. All the skits were well received by the young man and his father, who sat through most of the event with the most wonderful look of joy on his face.

We closed the celebration with a time of prayer for the son and then spent nearly an hour having refreshments and talking about the need for men throughout the world to bless our priceless young people. The following day, we put the two men on a plane to Zimbabwe to carry on with God's design for their lives.

TIME FOR A PRIORITY CHECK?

In light of the crisis that we face with our young people today, I want to encourage each pastor, youth leader, and member of a men's ministry to reevaluate their priorities. Please take time to think through your mission and goals for the coming years. Pastors, are you preoccupied with plans to build buildings and increase your church membership? Those are not bad things by any means; however, they are not what is closest to the Father's heart.

Youth pastors, are your thoughts consumed by ways to attract more "kids" to your services—and once you get them there, to figure out how to compete with secular entertainment? Again, these are not bad things to consider. But the reality is that you can never outdo the world's glitz and glitter, so why try? You have something so much more meaningful to offer.

Men involved in men's ministries, are you going to spend another year trying to get your life more together? Of course, we all need to strive to be more Christlike. But if you wait until you have perfected your walk of faith before you move into mentoring, you will have allowed countless youth to fall by the wayside.

We all need to awaken to the fact that we have a sacred responsibility to accomplish all that God has for us to do. Yes, we should build new buildings when needed. Yes, we should find innovative ways to attract new people to our services. Yes, we should continue to get rid of our own bad habits. However, if our pursuit of these activities leaves us without time, energy, or other resources to invest in our young people, then our priorities are out of balance. Men serving in any of these capacities may need to reprioritize and redirect their efforts to where they will do the most good for the kingdom of God. This means that we must add "looking after the fatherless young people" to the top of our list. Otherwise, we may drift into self-centered activities that only give the illusion of progress. But we'll be missing the will of God by a mile.

I am reminded of the evangelist who was asked about the success of his previous evening's crusade. When questioned about the number of converts, the evangelist mysteriously replied that two and *a half* people were converted to the faith. His answer momentarily shocked his listener. Regaining his composure, the inquirer then nodded his head knowingly, smiled, and gave his interpretation of the riddle.

"Oh, I get it," said the man. "You mean that you had two adults and one child come to the Lord. Hey, that's great! Why just last week we had…"

The evangelist raised his palm and shocked the listener again.

"No, you don't get it," he said quietly. "Last night, there were two children and one adult responding to the call. I consider the adult as a half because he only has half his life to live for the Lord. In contrast, I count each young person as a whole; they have their whole lives before them for serving God and others. "

Of course God can do amazing things in and through us no matter what age we are; he is always seeking us and loving us. Yet if there was ever a time to prepare and release this next generation, it is now. This generation will soon be the leaders of this world. They will make the laws. They will decide what is right and what is wrong. They will accept or reject God's ways in their homes, communities, and nations. The world is ready to be changed by their ideas, vitality, and faith. Our churches are filled with thousands of young people with their whole lives to give. What are you willing to give to help make their lives whole?

One Boy at a Time

The black car slowed to a stop at the railroad crossing near the edge of town, its passengers startled to see a young man walking down the middle of the train tracks. Storm clouds approached, goaded on by a cruel north wind. *Where would someone be going on such a heartless night?*

Rain came in a whisper then with an angry roar, soaking the young man as he shuffled down the tracks. With his hands thrust in his pockets and head down, it was hard to tell much about him. His race and age were concealed by the night. The men heard the distant sound of an approaching train. The young man didn't seem to notice, although he was in harm's way if he stayed his course.

The driver put down his window and shouted, "Hey, kid! Where you going? Hey! What's the matter with you?" Without a backward glance, the young man continued to walk down the track. His lack of response angered the driver. "Hey! Get off those tracks! There's a train coming! Don't be stupid! Hey, kid, grow up!"

The man in the passenger seat tried to calm the driver. "Easy, man. It's nothing to get upset about. You know young people today just don't listen. If he really wanted help, he'd ask for it. I'm sure he'll move before the train gets here." He glanced at his watch. "Come on, let's get going. We've already missed the start of the game. Hey, maybe at halftime we could call some agency or something. You know, somebody who gets paid to handle situations like this…"

The young man's thin figure was nearly hidden by the night's blackness as each step took him farther from the men. Only an occasional flash of lightning gave proof that he was still there. From the backseat came the third man's quiet voice: "We can't just leave him."

"What can we do?" snarled the driver. "We tried to help him and it didn't do any good!"

"We can't just leave him," the quiet man responded. "He's headed the wrong way. I'm getting out."

"Now, don't rush into this," soothed the man in the front passenger seat. "He's just one kid. You know, he could be dangerous, too. Let's drive on. If you want, we can come back later."

"No," said the quiet man as he stepped out of the car and into the stormy night. "I've got to reach him."

"You're a fool!" fumed the driver. "I've got better things to do than wait for some dumb kid who hasn't got enough sense to get out of the rain. We're outta here!"

The black car sped away, leaving the quiet man alone in the storm. In the distance, he could barely see the young man. Doubts bombarded his mind: *Did I do the right thing? What if he is dangerous? What if he won't listen? What if…?*

His questions were cut short by another blast of the train whistle. Beneath his feet, he could feel the rumble of the train as it approached. Adrenaline surged through his body as he began to run down the tracks, realizing that this was truly a matter of life and death. A warrior's prayer exploded through his clenched teeth. "Oh God, please help me reach him in time!"

His flying feet soon closed the gap between them, and he was within shouting distance. "Hey, hold up!"

The train rounded the bend and screamed straight toward them. The young man's frame was silhouetted in the headlight of the giant engine.

"Hey! Turn around! *Please!*"

These words seemed to break the spell that had clouded the young man's thinking. He suddenly stopped and turned to face the man pursuing him in the storm. In his young eyes were confusion, fear, and something that had been dormant for months—hope. Someone really *did* care!

His silent celebration came to an abrupt halt as he realized the train was just yards away. Its whistle screamed and the metal wheels roared out their final warning. Surely he had made a fatal mistake with his life. The young man shut his eyes and braced himself for the crushing impact.

But instead of jagged metal, he felt a strong hand grab his jacket and throw him out of the way of the train. Both men tumbled to a stop in the wet grass. The train flew past and mindlessly continued down the track. Soon the steel nightmare was out of sight.

Badly shaken, the young man spoke first. "Uh, thanks. I don't know what else to say."

The quiet man slowly responded. "You're welcome, friend. But that was a little too close for comfort."

After several moments, the young man spoke again. "Mister, I sure hated walking down that track. I just didn't know where else to go. It seemed better to go the wrong way than to go nowhere." His eyes pleaded for the quiet man to understand. "I don't suppose that makes any sense to you, does it?"

The quiet man smiled and tried to catch his breath. "Yes, Son, it does. Not too many years ago I walked down these same tracks. But I found a better way, God's way. If you want, I'll show it to you."

It didn't take long for the young man to respond. "When?"

"How about right now?"

They picked themselves off the muddy ground and began slowly walking together toward town.

"What's your name, Son?" asked the quiet man.

The young man hesitated for a moment and then replied, "My name's Jason."

Far in the distance, a train whistle screams out its warning once again. Someone else is on the tracks. *Whose son is it this time? Is he mine? Is he yours? Will someone reach him before it's too late? Will someone care enough to even try to reach him?*

Only one of these questions has a sure answer. *You* can be the one who cares enough to try. Throughout the world, countless young people walk down tracks that lead them the wrong way. These youth come in all different shapes, sizes, and colors. Some of them are rich; others are poor. In each case, there is a train of destruction hurtling toward them. Cynicism, despair, drugs, alcohol, HIV, gang violence, or perhaps suicide will destroy many of these precious young people if we don't intervene.

Some boys will live through these dangerous encounters and may even prosper later in life. However, many will die in their youth without ever reaching their potential. Others will be physically or emotionally crippled for life. Still others will drift from track to track without clear purpose or direction. These are the orphans spoken of in James 1:27. These are the fatherless ones without comfort. Can the lack of a father or father figure really have that big of an impact? If you are still not sure, here are some statistics from the National Fatherhood Initiative to help you decide: In American families,

- 85 percent of fatherless youths get involved with criminal activity,
- 78 percent of fatherless youths become high school dropouts, and
- an amazing 82 percent of girls who get pregnant as teenagers come from families where no father is present.

This bleak picture can be changed. The destruction of so many of our youth can end. But we men must come forth and lead our young counterparts along the proper path to maturity. One on one. Generation after generation. Our young men don't need famous figures they can worship. They need father figures they can love and who love them. Though our sons naturally grow in *masculinity*, they must learn how to become men of *maturity*. They need someone who has already traveled the road of manhood and is willing to show them the way.

The sacrificial act of mentoring our youth will change not only individual lives but our entire society. The logic is undeniable. The foundational building block of a godly society is the family, a husband and wife together, doing their best to raise godly children. It is painfully obvious that the departure from this model threatens to tear down our nations. But it is just as obvious that this trend does not have to continue.

When just one man, Jonah, walked through the city of Nineveh with a message of change, the city turned around. Imagine what will happen when thousands of godly men and women walk through our society with a message of positive change. When the older men encourage the younger men to follow them. When mentoring of the younger men becomes a way of life. Then strength will return to our cities and nations.

There is a move of God upon the earth today to restore things that have been lost or stolen. Good things. Family. Faith. Fatherhood. Mentoring. It is God's desire that the hearts of the fathers are turned to their children and the hearts of the children are turned to their fathers (see Malachi 4:6). This is achievable in our time.

The new millennium has seen a reawakening of men's spirits throughout the world. Near the turn of the century, over one million men gathered at men's events, such as Promise Keepers, men's ministries, and in local church groups in the United States alone. If each of these men commits to mentor just two young men in his lifetime and teaches them to repeat the process, the results will be incredible. When men catch the vision, we can turn around entire nations within one generation. Only one thing can stop us: failing to start.

This week—no, today—I solemnly challenge you to turn off the television, put away your business planner, and prayerfully find at least one young man who needs someone to help him enter into manhood. If you have a son, start there. If you don't, search until you find a boy who needs a man in his life.

Once you find him, begin to listen to, love, and lead that young man. Pray for and with him. Host a celebration in his honor. Affirm his journey to mature manhood. Take him places with you. Teach him the value of work, rest, and play. Make him laugh. Answer his questions. Hug him when he hurts. Show him the love of his heavenly Father. Teach him the Scriptures. When you consider the impact that a celebration and mentoring can have on the future of a young man who has no father or on the boy who has never been affirmed, you will realize that it is one of the best investments you can make in life.

Our opportunity to change the direction of an entire generation is very real. Consider that just one or two men can positively change the course of their church simply by blessing the young men in the congregation. A small handful of men can direct the course of their community by hosting celebrations and mentoring the young men from their neighborhood. If time constraints, expense, or large numbers of candidates present problems, concerned mentors can host a group celebration where numerous young men are blessed. The variations on this rite of passage are many, as we have seen in previous chapters. It just takes a few men to accept their God-given calling as mentors. It just takes *you* to do it.

We need to set aside the incessant demands of the day in order to secure something of eternal value for the young men around us. We need to accept the mentor's mantle. Today, choose to do for other young men what you wish someone had done for you when you were a boy. Choose to turn a generation of boys into godly men, one boy at a time.

ABOUT THE AUTHOR

Brian D. Molitor is the chief executive officer of Molitor International and founder of The Power of Agreement Network. These organizations specialize in consulting and training in interpersonal relationships, organizational development, team building, problem solving, and leadership coaching. He has produced and hosted numerous television programs on various topics including family building, writes business columns for several magazines, and produces numerous training manuals, videos, and audiotapes that are used by people in business, ministry, government, and families throughout the world. Molitor is also the author of *The Power of Agreement.*

Before his present career, Molitor worked as director of a residential camp for troubled youth and was the director of a statewide men's prison ministry, ministering to young men in particular. He and his wife, Kathleen, are the parents of four children: Christopher, Steven, Jenifer, and Daniel. As a dad, Molitor enjoys coaching a number of sports, including his sons' basketball and junior-league football teams. He and his family live in Michigan.

You may contact Brian by using any of the following methods:

Web site: http://www.powerofagreement.com
E-mail: passages@powerofagreement.com
Toll-free telephone: (866) 218-5009
Fax: (517) 835-9993